PEYTON MANNING

Recent Titles in Greenwood Biographies

PEYTON MANNING

A Biography

Lew Freedman

GREENWOOD BIOGRAPHIES

GREENWOOD PRESS
An Imprint of ABC-CLIO, LLC

A B C ☕ C L I O

Santa Barbara, California • Denver, Colorado • Oxford, England

Library of Congress Cataloging-in-Publication Data
Freedman, Lew.
    Peyton Manning : a biography / Lew Freedman.
        p.   cm.
    Includes bibliographical references and index.
    ISBN 978-0-313-35726-8 (hard copy : alk. paper) — ISBN 978-0-313-
35727-7 (ebook)
    1. Manning, Peyton. 2. Football players—United States—Biography.
Quarterbacks (Football)—United States—Biography. I. Title.
GV939.M289F74 2009

    796.332092—dc22
    [B]   2009016111

13 12 11   2 3 4 5

This book is also available on the World Wide Web as an eBook.
Visit www.abc-clio.com for details.

ABC-CLIO, LLC
130 Cremona Drive, P.O. Box 1911
Santa Barbara, California 93116-1911

This book is printed on acid-free paper ∞

Manufactured in the United States of America

CONTENTS

Photo essay follows page 66

SERIES FOREWORD

In response to high school and public library needs, Greenwood developed this distinguished series of full-length biographies specifically for student use. Prepared by field experts and professionals, these engaging biographies are tailored for high school students who need challenging yet accessible biographies. Ideal for secondary school assignments, the length, format and subject areas are designed to meet educators' requirements and students' interests.

Greenwood offers an extensive selection of biographies spanning all curriculum related subject areas including social studies, the sciences, literature and the arts, history and politics, as well as popular culture, covering public figures and famous personalities from all time periods and backgrounds, both historic and contemporary, who have made an impact on American and/or world culture. Greenwood biographies were chosen based on comprehensive feedback from librarians and educators. Consideration was given to both curriculum relevance and inherent interest. The result is an intriguing mix of the well known and the unexpected, the saints and sinners from long-ago history and contemporary pop culture. Readers will find a wide array of subject choices from fascinating crime figures like Al Capone to inspiring pioneers like Margaret Mead, from the greatest minds of our time like Stephen Hawking to the most amazing success stories of our day like J. K. Rowling.

While the emphasis is on fact, not glorification, the books are meant to be fun to read. Each volume provides in-depth information about the subject's life from birth through childhood, the teen years, and adulthood. A thorough account relates family background and education, traces personal and professional influences, and explores struggles, accomplishments, and contributions. A timeline highlights the most significant life events against a historical perspective. Bibliographies supplement the reference value of each volume.

INTRODUCTION

From the moment Peyton Manning arrived in the National Football League at the start of the 1998 season, he has been a numbers machine, completing passes at a dazzling rate and throwing touchdowns at a pinball-machine clip. Football fans, Indianapolis Colt teammates, and NFL foes alike have been in awe of what Manning's right arm has wrought.

There was no waiting period before the 6-foot-5, 230-pound quarterback blossomed. He was an instant star. Manning had been an All-American passing leader for the University of Tennessee and was the number 1 overall draft pick in the NFL collegiate draft, so there were high expectations from the first moment that Manning pulled on his blue and white Colts uniform. Yet while stardom is often predicted of rookies, there is usually a break-in period, an adjustment period, and this is especially true for quarterbacks.

Manning defied the odds by stepping into his role immediately to lead the Colts' offense. He did make his share of newcomer mistakes, but the majority of the time he was as poised as any veteran. It had been said that growing up as the son of Archie Manning, a former collegiate and professional star, in a family of quarterbacks and football players, Peyton Manning was as ready-made for the NFL as any player could be. Overnight, he proved the sages correct.

The apprenticeship of a National Football League quarterback is normally considered to rival the education of a medical doctor, with the belief that neither is qualified to operate safely until a few years pass. While playing football can be downplayed with the phrase "It ain't brain surgery," stepping into the role of professional quarterback does take some brain power. It also requires athleticism, an ability to comprehend the swift action on the field, sharp reaction time to changing circumstances, and supreme confidence.

Manning started his first game as a professional and all sixteen the Colts played during his rookie year of 1998. In the pros, that is considered akin to being thrown into the swimming pool to learn how to swim and an achievement in itself for a first-year player. For a quarterback it is also seen as an achievement magnified several times because the position is regarded as the most complicated to play in the sport and one of the most difficult to play in all of sports.

There were Manning growing pains, with the usual complement of mistakes committed, but the same young man who threw 28 interceptions that season also completed 26 passes for touchdowns. The same young man who was steamrolled for a truckload of sacks by voracious defenses threw for 3,739 yards. He took advantage with his smarts and took his lumps from his inexperience, but Manning never took a step in retreat.

Almost overnight, Manning was promise fulfilled, the dream draft pick morphing into a brilliant All-Pro, the player who had been on a self-propelled, years-long journey to glory finding the Promised Land as he had hoped. If Manning was almost too good to be true as a player, a leader, an athlete, and a self-effacing personality, he was also not one to rest on swiftly acquired laurels. Manning barely paused with the engine running to soak in the satisfaction of reaching a long-cherished goal. Rather, he immediately emphasized to himself and those around him that he had much more work to do, that he had to improve his skills to keep on getting better.

The easy thing would have been to take a breather, to relish a job well done. It was only when Manning eschewed such a choice that outsiders truly began to understand that he was motivated by more than money or fame, that he was a perfectionist who sought to become the best at his position, that he sought to improve in order to carry his team on his shoulders, that his inner urge was all about winning.

In the years that followed Manning's impressive rookie year he did work around the clock and around the calendar to become a better quarterback. By the autumn of 2004 Manning was reaching new heights, new levels of on-field accomplishment. That season Manning set a new NFL record with 49 touchdown passes. Three-fourths of the way into the season, after a 41-10 Colts thumping of the Chicago Bears at Soldier Field in Chicago, the football world began realizing just what type of magic Manning was making. After tossing four touchdown passes against the Bears on a cool November day, he had put up 35 in 10 games.

Even Manning's teammates and coaches were nearly reduced to giggles watching him. They admitted he was so good he was spoiling them to the point they even took his performance for granted. "You really do," said Colts coach Tony Dungy. "We kind of get so we expect these 70 percent completion days, four touchdowns," Dungy said. "We kind of ho-hum it."[1]

Manning was blessed with great receivers, such as stars Marvin Harrison and Reggie Wayne, and the way the group bonded and worked together, moving the ball downfield, seemingly at will, boggled the rest of the league. These Colts picked apart defenses with efficiency and found holes in defenses that no one else could spot with a microscope. "He makes it real easy for us," Wayne said of his quarterback.[2]

Game after game, week after week, the Colts, with Manning in charge, were providing a show that filled the air with footballs and left fans wonder-struck. The only one who wouldn't admit that the Colts made all of their scoring in the aerial circus appear effortless was Manning, who repeatedly said nothing comes easily against an NFL defense. But he conceded something else: "We're just good at what we're doing now."[3]

Manning added an NFL single-season-record 49 touchdown passes to his resume that season, but in the years since his excellence has come to be even more widely appreciated. He became a world champion and he became a world-class pitchman for products in TV ads. Once perceived as a nerd of a hard worker he loosened up in public, and when Peyton was joined by his brother Eli as an NFL quarterback and Super Bowl champ, they firmly established themselves as part of the first family of football.

Peyton Manning had traveled a long way from growing up in New Orleans known as Archie's son. By the time he led the Indianapolis Colts to a Super Bowl championship in 2007, Manning had become the best-known football player in the game and one of the most famous athletes in the United States.

NOTES

1. Lew Freedman, "QB on Pace to Make History," *Chicago Tribune*, November 22, 2004.

2. Ibid.

3. Ibid.

TIMELINE: EVENTS IN THE LIFE OF PEYTON MANNING

1976	Born on March 24 in New Orleans, Louisiana
1976–84	Learns about football from watching father Archie star in the NFL with the New Orleans Saints and Minnesota Vikings.
1976–94	Develops love of college football listening to old University of Mississippi tapes of his father's games and by attending Ole Miss games with mother Olivia and father Archie.
1991	Becomes starting quarterback for high school team Isidore Newman High in New Orleans where top receiver is brother Cooper.
1992	Cooper, a member of the University of Mississippi team, is discovered to have a congenital narrowing of the spine and must give up football.
1993	Completes high school as three-year starting star quarterback and is recruited by colleges from all over the country.
1994	Surprises football world by selecting the University of Tennessee for college football instead of the University of Mississippi, partly because Cooper can no longer play.
1994	Due to injuries to two other quarterbacks, Manning becomes the starting quarterback for the Volunteers during his freshman year.
1995–96	Leads Tennessee to a high national ranking and is named Most Valuable Player in the Citrus Bowl.

1996   A Tennessee trainer accuses Manning of dropping his trousers in the athletic facilities as part of a lawsuit charging sexual harassment.

1997   All-American Manning completes his college degree in three years and is universally expected to turn pro. However, he decides his heart is still with Tennessee and opts to complete his four years of NCAA eligibility instead of going pro. Tennessee wins Southeastern Conference title and earns a chance to claim the national championship with a game against Nebraska in the Orange Bowl. In a surprise vote, Manning is out-pointed for the Heisman Trophy by Michigan's Charles Woodson.

1998   Tennessee loses to Nebraska in the Orange Bowl. Manning is taken number 1 overall in the annual NFL draft by the Indianapolis Colts and as a rare full-time starting quarterback sets five NFL rookie passing records.

1999   Manning is named to Pro Bowl for first time.

2000   Throws for 430 yards and four touchdowns against Jacksonville Jaguars on *Monday Night Football*. Records first single-game passer rating of 158.3 versus New England Patriots.

2001   Frequently changing plays at line of scrimmage, Manning and Colts use no-huddle offense for first time.

2003   Manning is named Most Valuable Player of the NFL for the first time.

2004   In April, brother Eli is the number 1 overall pick in the NFL draft by the San Diego Chargers and in a prearranged deal is traded to the New York Giants. At the end of the season Peyton Manning is named Most Valuable Player for the second year in a row.

2007   Quarterback Manning leads the Colts to victory in February at end of season over Chicago Bears and is selected as Most Valuable Player of Super Bowl XLI.

2008   Eli Manning is selected as the Most Valuable Player of Super Bowl XLII.

2008   Manning suffers first major pro injury in July, has knee surgery, and cannot participate in training camp.

2008   Despite sore knee, Manning starts season in September at quarterback and plays every game.

2008   In December, Manning becomes the second player to ever win three NFL Most Valuable Player awards.

Chapter 1

SUPER BOWL KING

The rain poured down on unroofed and unprotected Dolphin Stadium, but Peyton Manning ignored the drenching drops as he piloted his Indianapolis Colts up and down the increasingly chewed-up grassy field. On this day, February 4, 2007, Manning was like a farmer trying to nurture his crop, so it was a good rain.

For three-and-a-half hours, in front of 74,512 witnesses to Super Bowl XLI, Manning played his favorite sport with a poker face, making decisions, adjusting to weather conditions, firing bullet passes to his receivers. Yard by yard as the Colts ate up the turf leading to touchdowns, second by second as the clock ticked down, the all-star quarterback inched his way closer to the dream that had driven him since he was a little boy.

The football team he led was closing in on the world championship, far enough ahead over the Chicago Bears to see the goal within reach, yet not so far enough ahead that victory could be taken for granted. With 11 minutes and 44 seconds remaining in the fourth quarter, the television cameras found Manning sitting on the Colts' bench. He wore a team baseball cap and had a cape draped over his shoulders to ward off the raindrops.

The Colts, a team that had not won a championship in 36 years, were leading 22-17. They were on the right side of the score, but were less than a touchdown ahead. One drive, one smooth touchdown pass or breakaway run by the Bears, even if it was a fluke, could easily drop them behind. Games turned on singular plays, a fumble, an interception, a long bomb pass, like that all of the time in the NFL. The Bears had possession of the ball as Manning watched intently. Once in a while he futilely brushed a towel across his face to absorb the rain.

Rex Grossman, the Bears' quarterback, was Manning's counterpart, the signal-caller for the opposition. Grossman was not nearly as accomplished a leader as Manning. He didn't have either the statistical credentials or the track record of bringing his team back from deficits. But it was prudent to worry anyway. The dream was so close the Colts could taste it, but an abrupt change in the game could make that taste bittersweet. As the Bears tried to spoil the day, tried to claim their own championship 22 years after bringing home their last trophy, Manning stood up on the sideline, his facial expression serious, his arms folded.

Grossman was out there in the hard rain pitching. He tried to hit a receiver downfield, but Colts defensive back Kelvin Hayden plucked the ball out of the air, darted and dashed and ran the crushing interception back 56 yards for a Colts touchdown and the clinching Indianapolis points. A look of determination creasing his face, Manning pumped his right arm as a minor celebration for points that would make his life easier. After the extra point, the Colts led 29-17, and the Bears needed two scores in a hurry to catch up. Manning and Indianapolis had a remedy for that.

Any professional football team with Peyton Manning at the helm is going to be a passing team. With Manning's arm strength and quarterbacking savvy a coach who wasted such abilities would be destined for the unemployment line swiftly. Yet Manning and the Colts—despite a passing attack that made their Hoosier fans ooh and ah regularly—had long ago learned that they could not capture the NFL's biggest prize without a balanced offense.

The Colts had relied on star running back Edgerrin James as an equalizer. Prior to this season, however, James became a free agent and joined another team. There was much hand-wringing among Colts administrators and Colts fans about how the power-back James could be replaced. The solution proved to be double-edged. James was a workhorse along the lines of Earl Campbell, one of the bullish greats of the past who could haul runners through the line on his back when necessary. The Colts did not find another James, but instead replaced him with two backs, alternating rookie Joseph Addai and Dominic Rhodes, and blending their talents. The idea proved to be the prototype for an NFL offensive change and soon several teams tried out a two-back approach.

In the closing minutes of the Super Bowl, when the main aim of the Colts' offense was not for Manning to find a roving Marvin Harrison for another pass deep downfield but to waste time to prevent the Bears from getting any additional chances to score, it was Rhodes and Addai who kept the chains moving for first downs. Manning's white helmet with the blue horseshoe had scratches on its crown, as if Bears defensive players seeking to sack him really did have the claws of the growling grizzly they were named after, but mostly he eluded them.

Manning's drumbeat speech of how it is never easy to score on an NFL defense (yet doing it) might well be a parable for how challenging it had been for the Indianapolis Colts to progress from beaten-down franchise to Super Bowl contender. The Colts' history was checkered. The predecessor Baltimore Colts owned much of the club's positive history, winning what was known as the "greatest game ever played" when they defeated the New York Giants for the NFL title in 1958. The Baltimore Colts were a superior team under Don Shula. The Baltimore Colts were powerfully identified with the revered Johnny Unitas, the quarterback who Manning surpassed in team records but not necessarily in greatness to all minds (including, seemingly, his own).

The Colts' origins dated back to 1947, but the Colts' connection to Indianapolis was much more recent—1984—and forever tainted in some minds because the team was spirited out of Baltimore in moving vans under cover of night in a snowstorm when negotiations over building a new stadium broke down. The rage of betrayed Baltimore fans led to the establishment of a new team, the Ravens, in the city. Indianapolis kept the Colts name, but struggled to build a fresh tradition. They were coming off a 3-13 season when Manning, heralded as the savior and the man who could bring the town a title, arrived. Now Indianapolis and Manning were on the cusp of that hope becoming reality.

At the very end, the contest between the Colts and Bears turned into a game of keep-away, like the children's gym class game. The Colts wanted to hold on to the ball as long as possible and the Bears wanted it back, needed it in a hurry. Time after time, Manning took the snap from center, turned, and handed off. The running-back tandem did the rest. The Bears' vaunted defense could not stop either man and the Bears' hungry offense was relegated to the sideline. Addai and Rhodes did their jobs. They tucked the pigskin into their bellies, cradling the ball safely as Bears would-be tacklers tried to rip it from their grasps and set the ball bouncing free on the turf. All of those desperate attempts failed and each of the twosome's running attempts succeeded.

They churned out first downs to keep the ball in Indianapolis control all the while as the fourth quarter's 15 minutes evaporated.

The Bears spent their final timeout with 1 minute, 49 seconds to play. Chicago got the ball back with 1:42 to go, but the football was situated at the Bears' own 16-yard line. Not only did the Bears face marching 84 yards to dent the score, they had no timeouts remaining to aid their play calling, and then they would have to score still again. Barring a remarkable confluence of peculiar events, they were doomed. The Bears knew it. The Colts knew it. The Colts fans dancing in the Dolphin Stadium stands in their rain-soaked team jerseys knew it.

Manning was 30 years old, completing his ninth season in the league, and each tick of the clock brought him closer to the pinnacle of his career. In the NFL, more than almost any other sport, the greatest players have come to be defined in public debate by how many championship rings they have won. This is especially true for quarterbacks, the visible team leaders. There is no outright denial of a player's greatness, but fueled by sports talk radio at Super Bowl time at the end of each season, the topic of being a winner is analyzed and dissected. The argument had taken root that a Joe Montana must be a greater quarterback than a Dan Marino because Montana's 49ers won Super Bowls and Marino's Dolphins did not. All of this overlooked the issue of the supporting cast, but that fact didn't quell the talk.

If anything, the annually renewed discussion seemed more an example of how society's values had changed over the years. Those who belittled Dan Marino, who set the league record for most touchdown passes and yards gained, appeared to represent the school of thought that finishing first was the only thing that mattered, that merely being considered a terrific player and a Hall of Famer was somehow insufficient.

This point of view had trickled down to Manning. Year after year Manning's Colts won a lot of games. Year after year Manning threw tremendous numbers of touchdown passes and gained thousands of yards. But before 2007, he had not been able to lead his team into the Super Bowl. In a slugfest of sorts of their own, Manning and New England Patriots quarterback Tom Brady were sized up like Muhammad Ali and Joe Frazier. Manning often out-threw Brady, but the Patriots won three Super Bowl titles under Brady's leadership. Worse still for Manning, the Colts and the Patriots were both members of the American Football Conference. Manning had always tried to keep these confrontations impersonal, emphasizing that he had no individual rivalry with Brady. And he never allowed himself to become embroiled in discussions about his own legacy, about whether he would feel his career was incomplete as a quarterback if he did not win a Super Bowl.

The fact that the Colts and Patriots were both based in the AFC meant that frequently the main obstacle to the Colts' advancement to the Super Bowl was a showdown with the Patriots. The Patriots had won most of those important match-ups. That was not the case this year. It was Manning and the Colts, not Brady and the Patriots, representing the AFC in the Super Bowl. It was Indianapolis's turn. It was a chance that Manning viewed very opportunistically.

For most of his football life, Manning had been renowned for his preparation and study habits, learning the quarterback position, absorbing the quarterback position into his brain and bloodstream, and studying film hour upon hour to find weaknesses in foes' defenses. For Manning, every week was a film festival as he watched the equivalent of the entire *Godfather* collection on each team. It was in that spirit in the days leading up to the Colts' embarkation for Miami and the meeting with the Bears that he suggested all players should retreat into a sort of lockdown at the site. He pushed for rules banning all civilians from players' hotel rooms.

There are myriad stories about the distractions that attend a team's lead-up to the Super Bowl, particularly a first-time participant, from families begging for daddy's time, to friends' demands for tickets, to single players' enjoyment of the nightlife. Manning wanted none of that to interfere with his and the Colts' quest. It had taken years of effort to qualify for a Super Bowl. He didn't merely want to play in one, he wanted to win one. This one.

"This is a business trip," Manning said, "and I don't want any distractions. I don't want any crying kids next to me while I'm trying to study." Other Colts players got the message that partying was not on Manning's agenda, and they didn't all like it, calling the adoption of his restrictive plan "Peyton's Rules." But they accepted it. Manning well knew that it was his reputation on the line more so than any comparatively anonymous linemen and that it was his big chance to eliminate the harsh "can't-win-the-big-one tag."[1]

The Monday prior to the game, Manning took 20 teammates out to dinner—his treat. This was symbolic in more than one way. Manning was playing the role of team leader (it was not revealed if he sat at the head of the table). Manning had the richest contract, so if anyone was going to buy it was him. And Manning wanted to play up the elements of unity and sticking together. If anyone joked that he also wanted to keep an eye on the guys so they wouldn't get into any kind of extracurricular trouble, that thought was never voiced loudly enough to be reported.

In the final seconds of Super Bowl XLI against the Bears, several of the Colts linemen picked up a barrel of Gatorade and dumped the contents over the head and shoulders of coach Tony Dungy. The action had become a strange NFL symbol of victory, one of the few times players could take liberties with their authoritarian coaches. It harkened back to the ritual lighting of a cigar by former Boston Celtics coach Red Auerbach. When Auerbach fired up his stogie that meant his basketball team had won. The Gatorade soaking was a declaration of victory, too, an exclamation point on the action.

Dungy became the first African American head coach to take his team to the Super Bowl championship. Like his alter ego leader Manning, Dungy had sometimes been criticized for not providing a championship sooner. In an instant, although the Gatorade drenching seemed somewhat redundant on such a wet day, all of the almosts of the past were forgotten. When the game clock struck zero, the Colts were officially Super Bowl champions. Manning raised his right arm in a gesture of celebration and pumped his right fist. A smile of satisfaction permeated his face as he strode onto the gridiron to share the moment with teammates and accept good wishes from opponents.

Chicago Bears superstar defender Brian Urlacher was one of the first to congratulate Manning. As confetti dropped from the sky like extra-large, multicolored snowflakes, the players crossed paths on the field. It was pandemonium with the confetti limiting visibility, players from both sides bumping into one another, TV cameras rushing onto the field, and the coaches seeking one another out for a handshake. Like his old friend Dungy, Bears head coach Lovie Smith, who had once been the Colts' boss's assistant, was black and their teams' meeting represented the first time both teams in the game were coached by African Americans.

Manning and Colts defensive end Dwight Freeney, a ferocious pass rusher, embraced on the field. Within seconds, premanufactured Colts caps proclaiming them Super Bowl champs materialized on the heads of the victorious combatants.

Swiftly, a makeshift round stage with Super Bowl emblems emblazoned on its sides was erected on the Dolphin Stadium field for a postgame presentation anchored by television announcer Jim Nantz. Only a short while earlier Nantz's cohost, Phil Simms, the former New York Giants quarterback who had set Super Bowl passing records when his team won the crown, had mused, "You dream your whole life [of making it to the game]. In reality, it's even better than your dreams."[2]

Colts players lined up in two rows facing one another as if they were knights of the Middle Ages about to create a canopy with their swords. Instead, as one-time Colts coach Don Shula carried the Vince Lombardi trophy to the podium, the sweaty and muddied winners reached out and touched the silver bauble on its way by.

As he handed over the trophy, National Football League Commissioner Roger Goodell gazed at Colts owner Jim Irsay and said, "This trophy represents the greatest achievement in team sports."[3]

Dungy got the next touch. He also took note of the milestone moment of becoming the first African American coach to lead a Super Bowl winner when not so many years earlier it was a challenge for any African American hopeful to even get an interview in consideration for such a job. "I'm proud to be representing African American coaches," Dungy said. "It means an awful lot to our country."[4]

One thing Dungy also put to rest for naysayers (not that he had been a doubter) was the notion that Manning was lacking for not having a Super Bowl title on his list of career accomplishments before defeating the Bears. "If people think you had to win a Super Bowl to know that [Manning was great] and validate it and justify it, that's just wrong," Dungy said. "But he's done it. He's got that behind him. I don't think there's anything you can say now other than this guy is a Hall of Fame player, one of the greatest players to ever play the game."[5]

At 6-foot-5, Manning, wearing one of the freshly minted Colts victory baseball caps and a similar Super Bowl championship t-shirt, towered over everyone else on the podium. During the game, Manning completed 25 of his 38 passing attempts for 247 yards. He had thrown just one touchdown pass. By the standards of his usual production the statistics were anemic. But his field generalship had moved the Colts into position for three field goals and a running touchdown as well, and his all-around performance earned him selection as the game's Most Valuable Player (MVP).

Dungy hugged Manning as he passed him the trophy. Manning raised the silver football in the air with his right hand, pursed his lips, and nodded. It was not an extremely demonstrative reaction. Consistent with most of Manning's postgame reactions, there was no gloating in this victory. Although interspersed with wider smiles, his facial expressions seemed to indicate more of an acknowledgment of a job well done, and his words echoed that feeling. Manning said that any number of the Colts could reasonably and fairly been chosen MVP that day.

"No question," he said, "and that's been our theme all year. We've won as a team. Everybody did their part. There was no panic. We truly won this championship as a team. It's hard to put it into words. We've stuck together. It sure is a great feeling."[6]

Manning did not hog possession of the trophy. Although he stood above his still-uniformed teammates, he leaned over one side of the podium and carefully passed the award down to them. Announcer Nantz could not resist a bonus comment: "One last handoff tonight by MVP Peyton Manning."[7]

Super Sunday had truly turned into one of the greatest days of Peyton Manning's life. It certainly had not rained on his parade.

NOTES

1. Michael Silver, "Peyton's Place," *Sports Illustrated*, Super Bowl XLI Commemorative Edition, February 2007.

2. *Colts' Road to XLI*, Post-Season Collector's Edition DVD (NFL Films, 2007).

3. Ibid.

4. Ibid.

5. Indianapolis Star staff, "Lone Mark against Manning Erased," in *Road to the Championship: Super Colts!* (Indianapolis: Indianapolis Star, 2007), 219.

6. *Colts' Road to XLI*.

7. Ibid.

Chapter 2

HIS FAVORITE TOY WAS
A FOOTBALL

Peyton Manning grew up in a football household, where the sport was livelihood even more than diversion. Like so many children, Manning was raised in a community where his parents had settled because of employment. Unlike most children, the work that brought the family to New Orleans was not the typical office or manufacturing job. Father Archie was a professional football player and was the number 1 draft pick of the New Orleans Saints, anointed as the National Football League's quarterback of the future in 1971.

More often a family business might be a neighborhood restaurant, a bookstore, or a shop of some kind. The family business in the Manning clan was football, but it was not a possession, a storefront, or a piece of real estate that could be willed or inherited. Nor did Archie Manning and his wife Olivia (born Williams) ever set out to raise a family of football players or attempt to raise anything but three well-adjusted, responsible sons. The Manning homestead was far from a football boot camp. Archie Manning actually sought to prevent his sons from participating in tackle football until they were older than other neighborhood children. He thought there was plenty of time for them to play the game on a more serious level after they turned 12.

The older Manning was not a believer in rushing kids into a sport, did not think it was right to train them for the pros when they should be out having fun with playmates, and did not think of his boys as miniature versions of himself who would go on to professional stardom. He was too busy being a dad and giving them the Christmas presents they wanted.

"Yes, I made videos of my kids playing sports from their earliest attempts," Archie Manning said, "and Olivia and I bought them all kinds of sports equipment and I played with them by the hour. But none of it was diabolical. I tried fishing gear, but they weren't interested in fishing. It wasn't football I was pushing, it was involvement."[1]

Archie was quarterback at the University of Mississippi. "Ole Miss," as the school is affectionately called, is also where he became a national figure and a local icon due to his excellence on the gridiron and his generally pleasant demeanor off of it. When Archie married the homecoming queen, Olivia Williams, it was very much like one of those royal weddings for the denizens of Oxford, Mississippi, the school's hometown, though instead of English accents the participants spoke with syrupy, down-home drawls.

Peyton Manning was born on March 24, 1976, two years after older brother Cooper and nearly five years before younger brother Eli. The fact that Archie Manning was an All-American quarterback revered for his football feats more than once colored Peyton's upbringing, decision-making, and others' focus on his own accomplishments. Whether burden or blessing—at times some of each—Peyton's choice to not just follow in his father's career but immerse himself at the same position on the field has linked them more strongly than any other athletic choice might have.

Football was what Daddy did. Football intrigued Daddy's sons. They watched games on television and when they got a little bit older they attended Saints home games and sat in the stands with their mother. They cheered for their father and his team, though that was often a fruitless endeavor since the Saints were among the worst teams in the NFL and could have used Huey Long's reputed capability of fixing the ballot box to eke out more victories.

Like any father, sometimes Archie took his sons to the office. No computers, secretaries, or telephones in the workplace. In his case work just happened to be Saints practices, usually on Saturday mornings before a home Sunday game. The team even put out doughnuts and milk for players' kids. Cooper and Peyton had the run of the locker room and the practice field. Naturally enough, they picked up footballs and threw them around. Archie used to laugh out loud at the cute maneuvers his son Peyton executed with a ball when he was a toddler and since he was a dangerous man with a video camera such moments were preserved.

"They have a tape of me when I was three years old," Peyton said years later. He said in the background his father can be heard shouting, "'Do your drop-back, Peyton, do your drop-back!' Football got into our life early."[2] Perhaps the role of quarterback did come naturally to Peyton Manning. (Many years later, when he was a professional, Peyton admitted to video existing of him taking tango lessons as an eighth grader and firmly saying the film was buried in Manning family storage. Yet it surfaced, was shown on a TV sports show, and is viewable on YouTube—thanks, Dad!)

Archie merely wanted to share time with his sons, not necessarily football time, but they often made the choice for him, clamoring to play football when they were still tiny tykes. Archie got down on his knees on the living-room floor in order to play football more at eye level with the two kids. An Archie running play involved him trying to score a touchdown by zipping along the floor on his knees while Peyton and Cooper jumped on him. It did not escape notice, however, that even by age four Peyton had excellent quarterbacking form when he threw the ball.[3]

If Archie Manning had never played professional football, never mind in the same region where he grew up, he still would have been a legend for his college football exploits. That is the period of his father's life Peyton completely missed out on, though he often heard his parents talk about how their college days on the beautiful campus were among their favorite times and how the Saturday college games against rivals like Mississippi State, Tennessee, and Alabama energized the entire community.

During the late 1960s, the National Collegiate Athletic Association (NCAA), the governing body of collegiate sport, was in one of its back-and-forth phases of prohibiting freshmen athletes from participating in varsity sports. As a result, Archie Manning did not compete for the Rebel varsity until he was a sophomore, when he won the first-string quarterback job. Mississippi was not one of the top teams in the league and Archie was frequently placed in underdog situations. One thing that endeared him to Mississippi fans was his uncanny knack for driving the Rebels to victory over highly touted teams. While at the helm of the Rebel offense, Manning, with his strong arm and quick feet, led Mississippi to three upsets of teams nationally ranked in the top five. He also was the cornerstone of a long-cherished, surprising 38-0 triumph over Tennessee. He earned national accolades and recognition as an All-American and set numerous school records from most touchdown passes to most passing yards. A song was written about Manning's football flair.

When Archie Manning's eligibility was completed, the school retired his number 18 jersey and in even a greater, though rather odd, tribute the campus speed limit was set at 18 mph. In the following years, Manning was chosen the greatest athlete in University of Mississippi history and was inducted into the College Football Hall of Fame.

As someone who was not born until five years after these glory years, Peyton Manning had not witnessed first-hand his dad playing college ball. However, when Manning was about seven years old a friend of his father's sent a gift to the old Ole Miss quarterback—tapes of radio broadcasts of games played during the 1968, 1969, and 1970 seasons. Curious, and with images of college football nirvana playing through his mind because of his parents' rhapsodies, Peyton took the tapes into his bedroom and played them over and over again. As the announcers shouted out the play-by-play he could imagine his dad throwing and running for touchdowns. Repeated listenings allowed Peyton to reincarnate his father's college football career and he developed a certain talent for mimicking the broadcasters as well.

"I listened to those tapes over and over like I was hearing them for the first time every time," Peyton said. "It was a kick whenever they mentioned his name. I know that sounds corny, but it was fun."[4]

Archie Manning was a tremendous all-around athlete and three different times he was drafted by Major League Baseball teams, but he had been a quarterback since sixth grade and knew what he wanted to be and to do. "Counting the mental requirements with the physical, quarterback is by far the most demanding position in all of team sport and undoubtedly the most glorified," he said. "For me, the challenge of playing quarterback was as thrilling as it was daunting."[5]

The nearby New Orleans Saints were one of the bottom-feeders of the National Football League and the team's poor record allowed it to pick second in the annual college player draft when Archie was graduating. There was a period when the Saints were so bad they were ridiculed as the "Aints" and some fans wore paper bags over their heads at games to remain anonymous. The Saints plucked Manning with the aim of leading a turnaround. This was both good and bad news for young Archie. The Saints were located only a few hundred miles from Oxford and served as the region's team, meaning Manning would be in his comfort zone. However, the Saints' horrible track record meant that Manning was going to be thrown to the lions, and not just the Detroit Lions.

A rookie quarterback rushed into service is often ground into mincemeat. Typically—and New Orleans was no exception—a team that picks high enough in the draft to obtain a star quarterback has few other weapons. This includes the type of offensive line that can protect a young quarterback. The result for Manning was often grisly. He was frequently on the run from 280-pound tackles determined to sack him. A pocket quarterback by inclination, he was often forced to throw while trying to save himself from demolition. It was wise for Manning to keep his life insurance payments up to date as squadrons of frothing pass rushers pursued him with the notion of ruining his health. Both Manning and the Saints suffered from growing pains.

Olivia Manning said that during those calamitous seasons when she took Cooper and Peyton to games (probably when they were seven and five-ish) fans in the Superdome often booed the team and her husband when he couldn't get the offense rolling. Rather than being offended by their daddy being insulted, the two boys didn't really understand the situation, she said. "During one game the boos were upsetting Olivia until she turned around and saw Cooper and Peyton booing, too," Archie said. "They thought it went with the territory."[6]

Failure to score, failure to win, and failure to move the offense did mean boos were expected, whether the boys comprehended the gesture or not. But Peyton took something else from his father's on-field difficulties which he catalogued and filed away for later, when he was a quarterback on a stage much larger than just tossing the ball around with his brother.

"There were a lot of days when he got beat up on the field and the Saints played badly, but he signed every autograph, he did every single interview and that's what it's all about," Peyton said. "He never brought his sorrows home, either. When he came home to the family, you'd thought he had just won the Super Bowl."[7]

Archie and Olivia had been small-town kids growing up in Mississippi, but Archie's job took them to the rollicking city of New Orleans. Although New Orleans was not New York, it was no out-of-the-way hamlet either. New Orleans has a personality unlike any other city in the United States, with its mix of cultures, Cajun influence, pride in its special regional cooking, and certainly one of the nation's largest and most unusual parties in Mardi Gras. Yet it was also southern and neither so distant nor so alien for Mississippians.

The Mannings moved to the plush historic Garden District of New Orleans and obtained a house spacious enough for rambunctious youngsters to play football indoors. Mom frowned a bit if the passes threatened lamps in the house as the kids imagined playing football in the Superdome, but the boys were more likely to break their own bones than to break her heirlooms. Whether it was their innate competitive natures or something else governing their actions, Cooper and Peyton fought all the time. They got into fistfights over football, board games, and petty arguments. They took sibling rivalry to the heights of the World Wrestling Federation.

Because he was bigger and older, usually Cooper won the confrontations. He might tackle Peyton and then pin him to the floor. Peyton would start to cry and Mom or Dad would have to break them up. "He was kind of a baby," Olivia Manning once said of Peyton as a youngster during this period.[8] Archie and Olivia were somewhat appalled by the intensity of the boys' scuffles. They didn't understand why just about every activity seemed to end with an outbreak of the Civil War. For several years, though, that's just the way it was.

"From childhood, we were competitive to the extreme," Peyton said. "We'd fight. He'd wrestle me down and let me know who was boss, and I'd get up and come back for more. When we got older and realized the damage we could do, we confined our disagreements to arguing."[9]

For the parents that recognition did not arrive a moment too soon. They were often exasperated by the boys' behavior. There were times when Archie felt as if he was a professional referee, breaking up lightweight boxers in clinches in the ring, and it was his job, not Olivia's, to handle the physical separations when he was around. He was absent for extended periods only near the end of his 14-year NFL career when he played in Houston and Minnesota and chose not to uproot his family.

"They fought like cats and dogs," Olivia said. "It scared me to death. If I was home with them and they'd start playing basketball, I'd almost want to get a broom or [water] hose to separate them."[10]

Archie added lectures to his duties of preventing Cooper's overhand right from connecting with Peyton's cheek and Peyton's left jab from connecting with Cooper's forehead. "The day you two can finish a game without a fight will be a great day in my life," Archie said. "You ought to be best friends. You don't know how lucky you are having a brother."[11]

Two, actually, but Eli was much younger, so as a baby he was pretty much out of harm's way. As the boys aged it was apparent that they had distinctly different personality traits. Cooper was a jokester, a risk taker, an extrovert who enjoyed partying and the nightlife. Peyton was intensely serious and studious, more likely to follow teachers' and coaches' directions, a straight arrow. Eli was quiet, laid back, more introverted, rarely revealing his true feelings. Being the youngest, Eli avoided the sibling wars. By the time Eli reached junior high, Cooper was in college.

The rlder Manning retired from pro football after the 1984 season. His best years, in New Orleans, were behind him and he hadn't played a full schedule at quarterback for a half-dozen seasons. He concluded his career with 125 touchdown passes and 23,911 yards gained. Capitalizing on his popularity with the Saints, he got a new job as a football broadcaster for his old team.

Archie Manning knew that he was raising a brood of passionate football players, but he never pushed his sons in that direction and always thought they should play all games, football included, for fun. He refused to allow them to even join a tackle football team until they turned 12. Not that any of the boys had made a secret of their desire to compete for their school. It was a given that they were going to go out for the team and not simply try out, but they were determined to make an impact with their ability. Cooper, Peyton, and Eli all inherited the football gene and if Archie was a cautious father in placing limitations on their earliest inclinations to play the game, nobody suggested their football skills came from Olivia.

The Manning children were enrolled at the Isidore Newman School in New Orleans. This private school offered education from kindergarten through high school. Isidore Newman was not a sports superpower. Although it fielded a team, the school had no reputation whatsoever in football.

One of Peyton's earliest football/life lessons that showed he would not be able to demonstrate the same type of hardcore critiques that he was used to exchanging with Cooper occurred when he was 12. As a member of the Isidore Newman basketball team Peyton called out his coach after a loss, blaming him for doing a poor job leading the team. Archie promptly bundled his middle son into the car and drove him to the coach's home—where Peyton delivered the required apology.[12]

The hatred of losing, the competitiveness that was so much a part of his makeup, had not diminished, but perhaps rather intensified now that Peyton was playing team sports at a higher level than a pickup game. That trait was not going to go away, but the message his dad sent was that there was a time and a place to use it wisely.

As the boys matured and their talents developed, it was clear that Cooper and Peyton were among the best athletes in their school. They enjoyed other sports, but they loved football and eventually they shared the same lineup for the same team. Cooper, unlike his father and two brothers, was not a quarterback, but evolved into a wide receiver. This was the catalyst that brought Cooper and Peyton together, that turned them into partners instead of rivals. When Peyton was a sophomore at Isidore Newman he won the starting quarterback job. That meant his key receiver was Cooper. They were now on the same page with the same goals and became a stunning tandem, moving the ball downfield and scoring touchdowns.

If Cooper was a free spirit (he would have been the first to jump in a car and high-tail it to Woodstock if he had been older), Peyton would be first in line to memorize the playbook, even if that meant staying home on a weekend night. It was no coincidence that Peyton earned higher grades in school than Cooper. Whether it was Xs and Os in football or other formulas in geometry, Peyton was going to attack the assignment. Cooper might try to skate by with simply a passing grade. He took the passing game much more seriously, but he also always knew that his brother would have a more astute grasp of it.

"I don't think there's ever been anyone more driven than Peyton," Cooper said. "He's always been wired. Whether it was football or pickup basketball, he wanted to be the man in charge. That's his nature. Always has been."[13]

It was a little bit later in life that Cooper and Peyton took note of each other's dominant traits and, rather than either belittle or hold them in contempt, the brothers developed an appreciation for them. They used the extreme ways in which they were different to salt and pepper their own personalities. "Peyton helps me get serious," Cooper said years after they were out of high school, "and I keep him loose."[14]

For all of their childhood battles, it was no secret that Peyton looked up to his big brother. For all of their professed love of football, Peyton admitted later that if Cooper had chosen to emphasize high school baseball over football, there was a very good chance he would have become a first baseman or outfielder rather than a quarterback. But Cooper, like his father, was a football player first. Just not a quarterback. Even though everyone else in his immediate family other than his mother did time behind center, it was not a role Cooper felt comfortable with. He even had a brief chance to confirm that when Isidore Newman called upon him to fill in at the position briefly because of player injury. He did so, but Cooper announced then and there that his quarterbacking days were over.

By the time Peyton advanced to the varsity to save his brother from any threat of being required to heave the pigskin, Cooper was a senior and the captain of the team. Peyton, with Cooper's compliance and assistance, urged teammates to practice longer and harder with the hopes of developing into a team that could make its mark in the state play-offs. This was the earliest sign of Peyton Manning as a football team leader. He was so devoted to the sport, so committed to success, that by force of personality he convinced teammates to put more time into pursuit of a common goal. Given that the team already practiced regularly under coaches' supervision, this was a little bit like going to the teacher and asking for more homework.

For the first time, skinny Peyton began lifting weights. He enlisted his brother into running extra pass-catching drills. There was doing the minimum to obtain a passing grade and there was doing work for extra credit to excel. Peyton chose the hard way and the harder-work way for sure.

During their one season playing together for Isidore Newman, the Peyton–Cooper Manning duo combined for 73 completions, 1,250 yards, and 13 touchdowns. For brothers who used to fight over everything from who got the last piece of cake to who got to watch their favorite TV program, it was a period of undiluted pleasure. Never had they had so much fun together. The team was successful with a 9-1 record and qualified for the Louisiana high school playoffs and the siblings realized they could be a lethal team by cooperating.

"For a quarterback, there's nothing like having your brother as your primary receiver," Peyton said. "You're on the same genetic wavelength. You know each other's every move. And you've been living in the same house together all your lives. How could you beat that?"[15]

Who would have guessed that the same brothers who had battered themselves bloody and made each other cry for years when they were younger would become such close-knit partners on the football field? Since they only had one overlapping year of high school at Isidore Newman, the experience ended too soon when they lost in the state semifinals. But the season also planted a germ of an idea for a Manning future together on the gridiron. Perhaps they could reprise this marvelous adventure of a year in a couple of years if they attended the same college and played on the same team again? It was no sure thing, but if they wanted to enough they could make it happen.

Cooper had not been a slave to Southeastern Conference game tapes of two decades earlier in the same dedicated way Peyton had become a student of Mississippi's games, but the stories his father and mother told about their enjoyable days in Oxford wooed him as well. When it came time to pick a college—Texas and Virginia were among other schools interested—the wide receiver chose to play for the Rebels, just like dear old Dad. There was always going to be a place on an Ole Miss roster for a son of the legendary Archie Manning, especially if he knew laces were up on a football. So Cooper went off to Mississippi, looking forward to running routes for the Rebels and soaking up some of his dad's reflected former glory. Cooper was not nearly as fast as many of the top receivers considered by the top programs in America, but he was 6-foot-4 and weighed around 185 pounds. He got open with his moves and if the ball was in his reach he caught it and hung on.

It did not surprise Archie that there was collegiate interest in Cooper. He had been aware for a long time that Cooper was an exceptional all-around athlete who could play many sports well and who above all, given his preference to play wide receiver, had good hands. He felt he could be successful at any number of things. "It all seemed to come easy for him," Archie said. "Peyton, on the other hand, was a natural quarterback."[16]

The idea of a brotherly reunion was floated, but it was a couple of years in the future, so nothing was etched either in stone or in scholarship commitments. Cooper was going to bulldoze his way into the first string on the Rebel depth chart. If the odds were against him because he was on the slow side for a college wide receiver (none of the Mannings was a threat to set records in the 100-meter dash), Cooper had a way of creating opportunity.

Only for once he never got the opportunity he sought. During his senior year in high school, even with his tremendous all-around performance and truckload full of catches, Cooper had dropped some Peyton passes that seemed easy to grab. Another time, when Cooper went to throw the ball, instead of a tight spiral he tossed a floater. He hadn't been able to grasp the ball correctly. He encountered a few similar problems during the Isidore Newman basketball season when the spin on his jump shot seemed to disappear.

During the summer leading up to his departure for college, Cooper underwent some medical tests, but nothing seemed amiss. In the fall, when he suited up for his first game for Ole Miss, Archie and Peyton were present. Cooper didn't play, but after the game a doctor told Archie that he was worried about Cooper's arm. Additional hospital tests showed that Cooper was afflicted with stenosis. The condition produced a narrowing of the spinal column that could lead to paralysis or eventually death.

Playing football, with the risk of getting hit the wrong way on any play, put Cooper at increased risk. At least one doctor suggested that if the condition had been uncovered earlier he would never have allowed Cooper to play high school football. Abruptly, Cooper's football career was over, and although the stenosis had been recognized without Cooper being harmed on a play, there was still some damage and he could not simply ignore it. Ultimately, Cooper underwent surgery and doctors discovered a blood clot. He had been at dramatically increased risk of paralysis. Far more was at stake than Cooper's chance to play football. The hours-long surgery removed the blood clot and Cooper did not suffer any paralysis.

On the day that Cooper was preparing for surgery, he handed Peyton a letter in a sealed envelope that he had been writing in fits and starts since he had realized that he was never going to be his brother's football teammate again. If playing football together had been a one-year shared experience that had brought the siblings closer, Cooper's illness and the letter he wrote to Peyton cemented a fresh level of mutual admiration and love.

In part the letter, which Peyton said he saved and still cherishes, read, "I would like to live my dream of playing football through you. Although I cannot play anymore, I know I can still get the same feeling out of watching my little brother do what he does best. I know now that we are good for each other because I need you to be serious and look at things from a different perspective. I am good for you, as well, to take things light. I love you, Peyt, and only great things lie ahead for you. Thanks for everything, on and off the field."[17]

There were fears and tears in the Manning household over Cooper's health, first of all, and sadness that he could no longer play football. But he recovered and continued his education at the University of Mississippi. And Peyton continued his own football education.

"With what happened to Cooper, I've counted every day of football since my junior year in high school as lucky," Peyton said.[18]

As a junior at Isidore Newman, playing without Cooper, the maturing Peyton threw 30 touchdown passes and led the team to the state quarterfinal playoffs. In the summer after that season, Peyton attended a football camp where he was observed by Saints head coach Jim Mora, who said, "If there's any better quarterback his age out there in the country, I'd like to see him."[19]

On another occasion, when Peyton and Archie visited the Saints' practice facility and the younger quarterback threw, Mora took his complimentary praise a step higher on the scale, saying, "The way he looks, the way he throws, I would have thought Peyton was a junior in college, not high school."[20]

During senior year at Isidore Newman, Peyton threw 39 touchdown passes and led the school to an undefeated regular season. However,

Isidore Newman was eliminated in the second round of the playoffs. Manning finished the three seasons of his high school career with a record of 34-5. He was named a high school All-American and was honored with many state and national awards. He was also pen-pals with just about every college in the United States that fielded a football team. Or if he was not exactly pen-pals with all of those coaches, then Peyton was at the least the recipient of boxes of junk mail.

From a distance, meaning outside the Manning household, most football people just figured Peyton as a chip off the old block, groomed by Archie to carry on the family quarterbacking tradition. The reality was quite different. Archie did not offer unsolicited advice to Peyton, but answered questions when asked. He was no Little League parent who screamed at his son from the grandstand. In fact, he tried to avoid watching Peyton's games from the grandstand altogether, instead choosing a sideline perch. He stayed as far away from Peyton's coaches as possible, too, so as not to interfere.

Yet Peyton saw his father as a resource, available at the dinner table, in the garage, or the family room to pick his brains. He said much later that he would have been foolish not to have sought his dad's input given his background and all of his college and pro football success. He had a live-in tutor who had been through it all before so why not take advantage of those free "master's degree" courses?

"It's been neat to have your hero in your own living room," Peyton said.[21]

NOTES

1. Archie Manning, Peyton Manning, and John Underwood, *Manning* (New York: HarperEntertainment, 2000), 180.

2. Mark Stewart, *Peyton Manning—Rising Son* (Brookfield, CT: Millbrook Press, 2000), 5.

3. Jeff Savage, *Amazing Athletes—Peyton Manning* (Minneapolis: LernerSports, 2005), 12.

4. Tim Polzer, *Peyton Manning: Leader On and Off the Field* (Berkeley Heights, NJ: Enslow Publishers, 2006), 19.

5. Manning, Manning and Underwood, *Manning*, 22.

6. Polzer, *Peyton Manning*, 24.

7. Ibid., 23.

8. Joanne Mattern, *Peyton Manning* (Hockessin, DE: Mitchell Lane Publishers, 2007), 10.

9. Polzer, *Peyton Manning*, 34.

10. Jimmy Hyams, *Peyton Manning—Primed and Ready* (Lenexa, KS: Addax Publishing Group, 1998), 61.

11. Polzer, *Peyton Manning,* 33.

12. Ibid., 34.

13. Ibid., 33.

14. Ibid., 36.

15. Ibid., 42.

16. Manning, Manning, and Underwood, *Manning,* 182.

17. Mattern, *Peyton Manning,* 12.

18. Stewart, *Peyton Manning,* 10.

19. Ibid., 8.

20. Polzer, *Peyton Manning,* 40.

21. Hyams, *Peyton Manning,* 13.

Chapter 3

BECOMING A QUARTERBACK

Archie Manning never planned to grow a quarterback (or two) under his own roof, but his own life served as the role model for his son Peyton. Although he was a good athlete who enjoyed playing a variety of sports, Peyton was far more involved in football than in basketball or baseball.

Peyton also naturally gravitated to the position of quarterback. He may not have verbalized it when he was young and chomping at his dad's restrictions against playing tackle football, but pretty much the only thing in life he wanted to be was a quarterback. Neither Olivia nor Archie overtly encouraged such thoughts, but Peyton wanted to grow up to be just like his father.

Between watching his father pilot the New Orleans Saints' offense and listening to those old Southeastern Conference (SEC) game tapes of Mississippi's outings under his father's tutelage, the notion formed in Peyton's head that this is how one leads a football team. It was Peyton's mother who noticed that when her middle son finally got to play quarterback for tackle teams that he walked back and forth to the huddle resembling no one else but Archie.

"When I moved up to 11-man teams mom said I'd come out of the huddle and up to the center with that same bowlegged stride that dad had," Peyton said. "Funny, but I never thought of it as imitation. It was, of course, and it shows the awe I must have felt. Dad's days at Ole Miss were life-shaping. For me, they were magical. If I could be a fly on the wall in time, I'd want to go back to when he played. Follow him around, do the things he did."[1]

There is no other way to put it: Peyton had a severe case of hero worship. In an era when the issue of whether or not young people should look up to professional athletes as role models is often publicly discussed, those athletes frequently reply that young people should look up to their parents. In Peyton's case he had his cake and could eat it, too. Dad was a professional athlete.

Archie and Olivia had no intention of raising professional football players. They just wanted well-adjusted, normal sons who made friends, played sports in school, got acceptable grades, and stayed out of trouble with authorities. Perhaps they were naïve, but they never imagined just how important football would be to their children, especially since they weren't pushing them.

The hunger was present in Peyton as a young man. He knew what he wanted to do and he wasn't afraid of the hard work that he realized it would take to succeed to make him a good quarterback. Rather, he seemed to relish it. In a children's book written about Peyton, a chapter titled "Born to Throw" mentions that Peyton always dreamed of becoming a quarterback.[2] If there is evidence to the contrary, that when he was a tyke that Peyton wanted to be a policeman, fireman, or cowboy, it has been buried by time. Almost from the start, it seemed "Football" was Peyton's middle name.

Football was Archie's dream and he made just about all of his dreams come true. But he didn't want to impose his dream on his kids. Despite his demanding job as quarterback of a professional franchise, Archie tried to come home for dinner every night that he wasn't traveling and spend time playing with the boys. Unexpectedly, the game they wanted to play the most was football.

"Dad always wanted to spend time with us," Peyton said. "We were the ones who always wanted to play football."[3]

During Peyton's elementary school years, he played a lot of backyard football, pickup games with no clock or officials. Archie was a compulsive family videographer, filming the kids at play and catching his wife off-guard in house-dresses or in other semi-embarrassing situations. He was a geek with a video camera but in the years to come the more proficient and active Archie became at making movies, the more he helped Peyton's talents improve. The first films of himself in football action that Peyton studied were home movies. It was not the quality of reproduction that coaches rely on, but it gave Peyton a fresh look at his play. Archie Manning had long before promised his wife that if they had boys he would not make them play football, but the more Peyton played, the more he peppered his father with questions. He viewed his dad as a live-in resource that he would be foolish not to use.

The type of information Archie Manning had stored in his head came from personal experience, from living through the gridiron wars in high school, college, and the pros. People sometimes talk about the difference between book learning and real-life experiences. In Archie's case he had acquired street savvy by living through games at all levels of the sport. When it became clear that Peyton wanted to play football for more than just amusement and hoped to become quite adept at the sport, Archie recommended a few things. He already admired his son's work ethic, but he advised watching as much game film as possible. He also told Peyton to be certain to look at the entire field rather than just following the ball.[4]

By the time he moved to high school football, Peyton was showing one of the traits that took hold deeply in him as a college and professional quarterback—a willingness to spend extra time learning the subtleties of the sport beyond the playing field. Football, many coaches like to say as a simplification, is about blocking and tackling. Fundamentally that is so, but Peyton was not content with the rudiments. He wanted to absorb the nuances of the game as well, hence his film study and what seemed to friends to become an all-encompassing preoccupation with the game.

"He's all football," said Walker Jones, a childhood friend of Peyton's from New Orleans. "I like football, but Peyton lives to play football and be around it."[5]

By the time Peyton suited up for Isidore Newman it was apparent he had the aptitude for the game. He was mentally suited to play football and to lead a football team. However, that did not mean he could do it. For every winning high school quarterback there are probably a thousand wannabes, kids whose desire is just as strong, but whose physical limitations whether in size or arm strength prevent them from ever becoming a starter, or even earning a varsity letter. Hunger is a powerful tool, but hunger combined with physical gifts sets the top performers apart. Peyton was on his way to growing into a 6-foot-5, 230-pound frame and he had the arm strength of a javelin thrower or a Major League outfielder.

What Peyton was still growing into—though in a hurry—was the unflappable demeanor that sets high-achieving quarterbacks apart. These are the quarterbacks who demonstrate poise in the huddle when calling plays, who never lose their cool when things are falling apart around them, and who are the leaders who feel their team is never going to lose until the clock runs out on them. With Peyton's intense study habits, his lifelong appreciation of the sport, his father's private mentoring, and his pure physical talent, by the time he was a high school junior Peyton looked like the second coming of family greatness to coaches, recruiters, and scouts.

Some football players who could not match Peyton's work ethic have joked that he was "born old," but the reality was that Peyton was "old school." He knew what he wanted and he went after it. He mapped out a life plan and was following it. Peyton had laser focus and he channeled it in the direction of his choosing—how to become a better quarterback. He wanted to turn Isidore Newman into a winner and he did that. He wanted to play SEC football, just like his father, and that was the next step.

Peyton did not harbor illusions about his capabilities. He knew he was a good quarterback, but he didn't pretend to be anything he was not. When he originally signed up for organized football he was listed as a safety. But he never played safety and he still hasn't played the first down of his life on defense or on special teams. If any coach was silly enough to waste Manning on defense at this point in his career, the man's locker would be cleared out faster than he could read the words on his pink slip.

Some great high school athletes have the ability to excel at anything and if they are destined for a pro career in any sport it is at least partially because they can run fast. Peyton knew he never possessed a sprinter's speed and always ducked out when he was going to be timed in the 40-yard dash (as all football players are). In his mind, it was a red herring. It didn't matter how fast a quarterback could come out of the starter's blocks.

"I actually was pretty fast up to about the fifth grade, even to the point of winning foot races with the other kids," Peyton said. "The whole business about 'time in the 40' is overdone anyway. A quarterback has to be nimble or he'll get killed, but he never gets down in a four-point stance and pushes off like they make you do for those speed trials. I was aware, though, that I needed to at least look good running. I used to work on my form just so I wouldn't be an eyesore going downfield on a busted play."[6]

There is little doubt that if Peyton Manning lined up on a track with Carl Lewis, Jesse Owens, and Usain Bolt that he would be last in the heat. But that is not the same as escaping downfield with fat-bellied,

300-pounders in pursuit. Peyton just didn't want those guys laughing at him while he chugged along.

The abrupt end to Cooper's football career had a dramatic effect on Peyton and his career. Peyton truly felt a new sense of responsibility, that he was representing his brother with his own football exploits. In the one year of high school that Peyton and Cooper had shared as Isidore Newman's primary passing game, the quarterback liked the sound of "Manning to Manning" over stadium loudspeakers. When he spoke about that season, even after his college days, Peyton said it was the most fun he had ever had playing football. One reason was that the Manning brothers were so good together that they even sneakily developed a private set of hand signals to communicate on the field, a system that not even their coaches were privy to. By establishing the secret code, the brothers could call an audible just between them if they saw a defense ripe for the picking.

When they were rambunctious youngsters, Archie hoped for the day when the two boys would no longer beat on one another and become best friends. That had finally occurred. Football brought them closer together than ever.

Then Cooper was felled by illness and they knew they would never play together again. While acknowledging that worse things happen to people's health every day, they still felt a palpable sense of loss since football was such a big bond in the Manning family.

"Cooper's condition taught me to appreciate life and to realize, hey, there's more to life than football," Peyton said. "Any play could be my last, so I try my best on every one."[7]

Peyton said from the moment his brother was diagnosed with stenosis, he has prayed for his good health every day. He also adopted the philosophy that his football accomplishments were Cooper's, too. "I feel I'm playing for Cooper," Peyton said. "I can't imagine having football taken away. Now the game seems all the more precious to me."[8]

The discovery of Cooper's problems with stenosis also indicated it was wise for Peyton to be evaluated thoroughly by doctors for the same problem. Medical testing showed that there was a slight abnormality in Peyton's neck but not a potentially life-threatening illness. He was cleared to resume playing football. Cooper had a second surgery a little while later and has some permanent hand and arm numbness but, except for contact sports like football, he can lead an unencumbered lifestyle.

Cooper's illness was definitely life-altering for Peyton with regard to his football career. Peyton, Cooper, and Eli grew up as University of

Mississippi football fans, their allegiance thrown behind the college program where their father starred. They also appreciated the pageantry and passion of the SEC as a whole, where Sundays are for one religion and Saturdays are for the seemingly contradictory secular religion of the college game. In the small southern towns where the large universities of the SEC are located, few things matter as much as how well the football team is doing, whether the Crimson Tide in Tuscaloosa, Alabama, the Tigers in Baton Rouge, Louisiana, or the Gators in Gainesville, Florida.

The sentiment for the home team in these communities, almost all of which are situated an hour or so removed from a significantly sized metropolitan area, is a common ground emotion for residents. The schools are the main generators of attention, employment, and population in the somewhat isolated communities of the region. As a rule there is little competition for fans from nearby professional teams and the roots of the rooting dates back generations. Mom and Dad might have gone to Auburn or Georgia and so might the kids and the grandkids. It might not be a good year for the cotton crop, but if the college crop consists of potential number 1 draft choices and the team is winning, conversation might still be upbeat, as in, "How 'bout them Dawgs?"

This was an area where the late Bear Bryant was better known than Alabama's governor—and better liked, too. It was an area where stadiums were named for legendary coaches and where institutional memory centered on the lad who scored the winning touchdown in the Sugar Bowl back in 1959.

The schools of the SEC belonged to all the residents of the community (and in some instances the state), not merely the students and faculty. The farmers and the doctors, the lawyers and the housewives, all had an ownership stake. Just like it was good for everybody when the bass were biting, it was a civic benefit when the Rebels or the Volunteers were winning. In a region where the greatest upheavals of the civil rights movement occurred and where societal change had been measured on the Richter scale, college football Saturdays in the proud SEC were something special people could still count on. Oh yes, integration had been an uneasy experience for those first changing the makeup of the football roster at Kentucky, Alabama, and Mississippi, but the times had changed and no one cared anymore what color the ball carrier was who was making all of those first downs.

For all of the changes, people were grateful that time had frozen on football Saturdays, that those early autumn humid days and nights were still decorated with the knights in hardshell helmets wearing short-sleeved jerseys with names on the back. With all of the computers and TV elements pouring their software into college football, occasionally hints were dropped that the best teams in the land were not members of the SEC, but headquartered in Columbus, Ohio, Norman, Oklahoma, or even Los Angeles. Despite those periodic blips and the recklessness of those judgments, the denizens of the South knew that their football was the best, that their SEC was the best league, top to bottom, in the nation. And despite the periodic lack of faith in distant cities, opinion always came around; it always came back to that fact. Those long-terms fans who inhaled the sweet fragrance of magnolia were right.

They knew in their hearts and from their upbringing what Peyton Manning picked up through his parents and by listening to the audio of ancient Ole Miss football games. Peyton had not grown up in small-town Mississippi. He had adopted the University of Mississippi's football team by osmosis. All of his senses (he later saw films of some of the same games he heard reported on the radio) were attuned to the doings at Vaught Hemingway Stadium. He even knew who Johnny Vaught was—the legendary Rebel coach who led the team in his dad's years. Heck, he even knew Johnny Vaught (who would die at 96 in 2006). Certainly, he knew that the 50,000-plus fans turned the stands into a sea of red with their jerseys and sweatshirts in support of the team on home Saturdays.

He might even have known that "Hemingway" was Judge William Hemingway, the long-time chairman of the school's committee on athletics. With the type of research Peyton was known to put into a topic, he might well have seen that fact in a football team media guide. It would have been incidental, however. For Peyton's entire life, Mississippi college football was paramount in his house. Not down-the-street Tulane or hour-away Louisiana State. When he visited the Mississippi campus, Archie Manning was still treated as a hero.

It was a foregone conclusion that Cooper and Peyton were going to take their passing game north to Oxford. Cooper was already on campus and on the football team. Peyton was two years behind and maturing into a stud star quarterback right before everyone's eyes. He had grown up with Ole Miss in his blood and that's where he wanted to play. Others could recruit him and they did, with mail and phone calls from all over the United States—coaches have to try—but many entered the process half-heartedly. They knew it was a waste of their time, energy, and resources. Peyton was following Archie and Cooper to the University of Mississippi and everyone knew it.

But no one reckoned on Cooper's illness. Cooper was enrolled at Ole Miss, but Cooper couldn't play football anymore. The days of Manning to Manning were over. Peyton was only a junior in high school when Cooper retired from football. Pretty much his entire football career lay ahead of him. He was still Ole Miss–mad. His college plan had revolved not only around his heartfelt ties to his dad's school, but also around the chance to spend two seasons throwing the ball to Cooper. The change in Cooper's status made Peyton think. It made Peyton look around. It made Peyton consider opening doors. The highway from New Orleans to Oxford was still a straight line on a map, but just maybe it was a highway that Peyton didn't want to drive. At the very least, he was less certain.

To those in the college football world, no prominent high school player in the country was more identified with a college than Peyton Manning. To hear that he might be receptive to playing football somewhere else cut so sharply against the grain of accepted wisdom that it was as surprising as it would be to discover there is no Easter bunny.

NOTES

1. Archie Manning, Peyton Manning, and John Underwood, *Manning* (New York: HarperEntertainment, 2000), 41.

2. Jeff Savage, *Amazing Athletes—Peyton Manning* (Minneapolis: Lerner-Sports, 2005), 10.

3. Mark Stewart, *Peyton Manning—Rising Son* (Brookfield, CT: Millbrook Press, 2000), 6.

4. Ibid., 10.

5. Ibid., 9.

6. Manning, Manning, and Underwood, *Manning*, 198.

7. Joanne Mattern, *Peyton Manning* (Hockessin, DE: Mitchell Lane Publishers, 2007), 13.

8. Stewart, *Peyton Manning*, 11.

Chapter 4

RECRUITING A HOT COMMODITY

Done deal. That's what the college football world thought. Archie's kid was the second coming, the boy with the golden arm, and he was on a fast track to Mississippi. The oldest son had already gone north to Oxford, so what more proof did anyone need? Peyton was going to follow in his dad's footsteps. That was the only thing that made sense.

Cooper believed that. Archie believed that. Peyton believed that. And every college coach in charge of an NCAA Division I football team believed that. And then Peyton changed his mind, or at least opened the door a crack, and said he might be interested in playing quarterback for someone else. It wasn't as if all of those people had been delusional, fooling themselves into believing something that wasn't true. Even Ole Miss coach Billy Brewer, who was friends with Archie, believed his quarterback needs were about to be fulfilled for the next quadrennial.

Peyton had grown up an Ole Miss fan, a devotee of the Rebels and all things Mississippi football. He had replayed all of those Archie Manning game tapes repeatedly and he kept up with the fortunes of the team in SEC play. With Cooper already in Oxford, playing as a wide receiver, Peyton was gift-wrapped for the Rebels, looking ahead to throwing passes to his big brother for two years of varsity play, or perhaps even three if Cooper red-shirted for a year, as is common. It was Cooper's illness and being forced to give up football that created the seismic shift in Peyton's thinking. Their dream of teaming up for the Rebels, Manning to Manning all over again, was kaput.

The abrupt change in Cooper's situation made Peyton re-evaluate. He faded back a few steps, just as if he was preparing to throw a pass, and surveyed the field. As such he was calling an audible in his own life from what had been committed to in the family huddle. Cooper was no longer part of the equation and that made Peyton question his thoughts. For the first time he began to think that it was possible to have a fun, fulfilling college football career at another school. Ole Miss was not out of the running, and pretty much everyone still thought Peyton would choose Oxford in the end. But whether it was reading coaches' letters, handling their phone calls, or studying team media guides, Peyton was going to go through the entire recruiting process. He was like a guy who had just broken up with a long-time girlfriend and was determined to see what else was out there before settling down again.

"I have no doubt that I would have gone to Ole Miss if Cooper hadn't gotten sick," Peyton said. "I really wanted to extend what we had in high school and the thought of our doing it where our dad played, and in a setting I had idealized for years, was practically irresistible. But Cooper's illness took the shine off."[1]

The sweepstakes was on. Once coaches realized that Peyton was a free agent in his mind, they lined up to woo him, to convince him that their school was the fairest of them all. Prized, coveted athletes (at least before electronic text messaging was inserted into the recruiting mix) often got as much mail as the president. Or so it seemed. Recruiting brochures and personal notes from coaches arrived by the bundle, enough to fill shoeboxes. The coaches' commentaries were football Valentines expressing love and devotion with all of their hearts, as well as offering scholarships for a free college education.

After he committed to the process, Peyton decided to glean as much enjoyment as he could out of it. That meant conversing with some of the most famous coaches in the country. That meant taking on-campus visits to see what life was like for the football players in the student body. The NCAA, the organization that oversees college sports, sets rules and parameters for college coaches when they plan to contact potential players. The rules do change regularly, but when Peyton first became eligible to receive telephone calls on August 1, 1993, he invited several friends over to share opening day with him.

Manning might have been talking on the phone with Bobby Bowden from Florida State when a call came in from Nebraska's Tom Osborne. He sometimes allowed one of his pals to answer the phone, acting as a secretary, to have the thrill of speaking with one of those coaches. At one point the phone rang and Peyton overheard half of an exchange that went like this: "No, Coach, he's not here, he's outside smoking a cigarette." Peyton panicked, fretful that a coach at a big-time program might write him off because he thought he was a smoker, and grabbed the phone out of his friend's hand. Gotcha! Another friend had telephoned from an upstairs line masquerading as a coach. The gang of friends, well understanding how serious Peyton was about these kinds of things, had played a successful practical joke on him.[2]

Typical of Peyton's approach to schoolwork and studying the playbook, he attacked the recruiting process with the same zeal and work ethic. He created index cards chock full of information about each school and filed them alphabetically. If the coaches were scrutinizing him, looking at the strength of his arm, the speed of his legs, or yes, if he actually smoked or not, he was doing likewise. Peyton's project, in addition to looking into the academic program (it was, after all, college), was to examine each school's win-loss records, its bowl history, the caliber of its receivers, and the team's history in developing quarterbacks and who might be returning to play for a few more years. Although he did not shy away from competition, Peyton might prefer not to attend a school that looked as if it was set with an All-American quarterback for the next two years. He had no desire to sit on the bench a minute longer than necessary. He did not expect to be a full-time starter as a freshman, but he did expect to see game action in his first college season. He wasn't demanding that he be given the keys to the offense immediately, but he hoped coaches would be open-minded enough to evaluate him on his skills, not his age and lack of experience.

Archie Manning, who had been heavily recruited as well, offered some basic advice to his son. He urged him to have fun with the entire process, to enjoy his trips to schools, and to simply make an informed decision. Archie, who had been living under the same roof as Peyton for nearly 18 years, still felt his son would decide to attend Ole Miss. But he didn't push Mississippi and he was determined to stand to the side and let Peyton make his own choice for his own reasons.

Interviewed by sports writers soon after the recruiting period opened, Peyton admitted he felt more like a guy in demand at a dance than overwhelmed by the bombardment of attention. "I'm enjoying it 100 percent," he said.[3]

Even years later, Peyton hadn't altered his viewpoint. He said he had found the recruiting process rewarding and pretty much a blast all around, from the travel to being able to chat with prominent college football coaches. "I loved the recruiting," Peyton said. "All of it. I read all the letters, answered all the phone calls. I read the media guides cover to cover. I loved my visits to schools. I loved talking with the coaches who came to visit me. I loved to question them. It was an incredible learning experience."[4]

The questions about Mississippi never ceased. Some writers probed Peyton's psyche, trying to see if he would be turned off by following his father to Oxford because they might relentlessly be compared for four years. Peyton had a ready-made answer. As someone who had already been playing quarterback for several years and had grown up in a household with a former All-American and pro who was the lightning rod for two different teams, he dismissed the query. "The way I see it, being Archie Manning's son, wherever I go, it'll be pressure."[5]

One of the theories behind frequent contact between coaches and recruits is "out of sight, out of mind." The thing that worries coaches most, even if a player has a marvelous time visiting the campus and tells the coach he loves the place and would like to play for him, is that the moment he goes home and is wooed by another coach he will forget all about those on-location emotions. Coaches believe young athletes are fickle and might change their mind on a whim or based on who whispers last into their ear. Coaches also know that even the most grounded athletes, A students mature beyond their years, during the recruiting process often feel as if their heads are spinning like the girl in the *Exorcist* movie.

All experienced coaches have suffered disappointment with a blue-chip recruit leaving them blue at the last minute, abandoning them "at the altar," so to speak. It's not because the athlete is deceptive, or doesn't like them, either. Oftentimes, the athlete just can't say no to different coaches who have been so nice for months. Oftentimes, the difference between saying yea to this school and nay to that school is extremely marginal. Each big-time athlete goes through the process once. Each big-time coach who has been around goes through the process hundreds of times. The kid's life plan is on the line, but the coach's job might be at stake.

Peyton Manning was a different animal than most recruits. He was so poised and mature, and had such a solid support network, that he was not going to be easily swayed, easily won over, or easily confused. Mississippi had a running head start and not a single college coach in America was unaware of that. But Peyton was true to his word and his own thoughts and that he had indeed opened up enough to consider alternatives. At one point, the younger Manning had between 40 and 50 schools on his list, still alive in his filing system.

Many coaches conversed with Archie. They were probing to get a sense of whether or not Peyton was really interested in them at all. He received phone calls from recruiters asking what schools were *really* in Peyton's top six selections. But Peyton was sincere. He had not reduced his prospect group to a small number. "He doesn't have a top six," Archie said. "He has a top 40."[6]

A top 40? Peyton sounded like disc jockey Casey Kasem playing America's Top Forty hits. The vast majority of college football hopefuls had nowhere near 40 or 50 schools interested in them enough to know their heights and weights. Peyton was on a first-name basis with a few dozen coaches and he was quizzing them.

Coaches who are used to getting one-word answers to questions when they interview a recruit found that Manning's plan was to interview them in-depth. Sometimes he sent them back for more research. As the months passed and the notion of having 40 schools on his maybe-list became unwieldy and unrealistic (there was only one Peyton and schools had to sign other quarterbacks), Manning sliced his finalist list to six schools. With the NCAA prohibiting more that six official visits to schools, recruits typically released lists of a half-dozen finalist destinations.

Although Peyton's announcement of his finalist schools was not accompanied by a drum roll, it could have been as far as most of the coaches were concerned, although for some the playing of "Taps" would be more appropriate. For fans of big-time college football, there really were no major surprises. It wasn't as if he was slipping in Slippery Rock as a possibility, or giving a nod to home area Louisiana–Monroe. For most of the hundreds of applicants bidding for Peyton Manning's college quarterbacking services, it was "Thanks for playing." They were out of the running.

The schools on Peyton's maybe-list read like the Associated Press Top 25 rankings. Michigan of the Big Ten was on the list and so were independent Notre Dame and Atlantic Coast Conference's Florida State, at the time perennial powers that had produced scads of All-Americans and Heisman Trophy winners, and appeared in season-ending holiday bowl games regularly. True to his allegiance to and fondness of the Southeastern Conference, Manning included three league teams on his list: Florida, Tennessee, and, of course, Mississippi. Compared to the recent achievements of the other five schools, Mississippi really didn't even belong in the group. The Rebels were not a regularly ranked team anymore, but everyone knew that they were under consideration, if not the frontrunner, because of the family link. Without

Peyton's heritage, the Rebels would not have been any more likely to be a potential matriculation stop than North Texas State.

There were no aftershocks, nobody dismissing any of the choices out of hand given their powerhouse backgrounds, proximity to Peyton's home, or involvement in the SEC. Of the six, some fans sagely observed that Tennessee was probably at most the sixth best choice. And they were sure-as-shooting positive when it came time for the final, final announcement that Peyton would be going to Ole Miss after all. Peyton had had his fun, he had entertained the staffs at traditional football winners, but really, when it came down to it, they figured Archie would grab him by the collar and give him what-for, sending him off to Ole Miss.

These observers might be optimistic season-ticketholders at Mississippi, sports writers with columns to fill who didn't really know the Mannings all that well, or the generators of recruiting newsletters who tended to believe that the rich got richer and that high school kids either didn't have minds of their own or weren't allowed to by their parents.

Just as highly sought athletes visit the campuses to take their measure, the head coaches and sometimes their offensive or defensive coordinators make pilgrimages to the recruit's home. Archie remembers Olivia cooking a pretty fancy dinner for almost all of the coaches and that on one night they entertained two groups from two schools with two meals. "Civilian" parents might be impressed by hosting Lou Holtz or Steve Spurrier at the dinner table, but the Mannings had already played in a different league.

When Ole Miss head coach Billy Brewer visited the New Orleans house, he made time to go watch Eli Manning's fifth-grade game before supping with the clan. Brewer knew the whole family well because Archie kept his ties with his alma mater. However, at dinner, Peyton began drawing offenses and peppering Brewer and one of his chief assistants with questions. It was difficult to tell who was more surprised.

"That night, Olivia and I got our first inkling that it might not happen; that Peyton might not choose our old school after all," Archie said later. "Peyton talked offense with Billy's coordinator using Olivia's linen napkins to write on, and you could tell it was awkward."[7]

Archie was saddened a bit, but remained consistent with his hands-off policy. Peyton had one more school visit to take. He was scheduled to visit the University of Florida in Gainesville, one of his three SEC finalists. The Gators were coached by Steve Spurrier, a Heisman Trophy–winning quarterback and Archie felt Spurrier's background might be the tipping point for Peyton. As he did elsewhere, Peyton enjoyed his journey to the Gator campus, but he made no commitment.

There is an official national signing day for schools recruiting athletes. It lets athletes declare their choice early, in the fall of their senior year, and have a relatively stress-free final high school year. As is common with athletes of Peyton's stature, where there is tremendous media interest in the player's destination, the Mannings scheduled a press conference on national signing day. If they hadn't, or if Peyton had chosen to delay his decision even longer, they would have been so inundated by phone calls the New Orleans telephone system might have collapsed from usage.

While he was pretty certain Peyton had doubts about Mississippi and that it wasn't going to work out for his son to follow him to Oxford, Archie wasn't sure exactly how Peyton was leaning. Knowing that Peyton was likely to get pestered by inquiring minds, either media outlets looking for a scoop or relatives or friends who were sure he would tell them first, Archie suggested that Peyton check into the nearby Hilton Hotel as a respite. The news conference was scheduled for Tuesday and father and son checked into the hotel on Sunday night.

Just because of its proximity and history, Mississippi did not skimp on the star treatment when Peyton took his official campus visit. Once he had opened up his search to all comers, the Rebels knew they were in a fight and they did not take Peyton's commitment for granted. Even Peyton conceded he got the "red carpet" treatment. On his Ole Miss tour, Peyton stopped in to check out the Rebels' locker room and was greeted by a new "Manning, No. 18" jersey in a locker. The coaches told him they would be happy to bring Archie's old number out of retirement for him, connecting two generations of Ole Miss football. A game tape was played for the following season's opening game that featured a play where Peyton threw a touchdown pass. Then Johnny Vaught, the aging icon of Mississippi football, who had coached Archie during his undergraduate days, arrived and added his voice to the proceedings. Come to Mississippi, Peyton, because we love you and we still love your dad, was the message. "It was all very touching," Peyton said.[8]

It was not really in Peyton's makeup to blow off a suitor because it didn't demonstrate it cared enough, but Mississippi covered that base sufficiently anyway. The Rebels showed they really, really cared.

So Archie and Peyton retreated to the Hilton to think and talk. It was not until Monday night, a full 24 hours after checking in, that Peyton told his father where he planned to go to college and what he planned to announce to the world on Tuesday. Actually, Archie had taken a walk and while he was out of the hotel, Peyton telephoned his mother and told her what he had decided—that he was going to attend the University of Tennessee rather than the University of Mississippi. When Archie returned from his neighborhood hike, Peyton gave him the news.

Peyton told both his mom and dad that he thought Tennessee was the best place for him, but if they strongly opposed that and believed he should go to Mississippi, he would do so. "[Archie] hugged me and smiled," Peyton said later. "He said, 'Don't even think about it, son. You go where you want to go. It's your life. We're with you all the way.' "[9]

For those who knew Archie Manning the person and the father, such a reaction would be no surprise. But for those who knew Archie Manning only as a Mississippi football hero, his graciousness, his failure to persuade Peyton to become a Rebel, was viewed as akin to treason. There was shock and dismay among the Oxford faithful and the repercussions were louder, more vicious, and more insulting than the Mannings ever imagined they might be. Archie was essentially the greatest football star in the history of the program and had been a long-time benefactor, raising money for causes and buildings on campus. His name was magic and wherever there were bodies of water in the Magnolia State it was presumed he could walk on them. No more. Soon enough Mississippi fanatics were hoping he might drown in one. The night in the hotel was one of peace, however, before Peyton's word spread.

On the morning of his press conference, Peyton telephoned the coaches awaiting the verdict. He had already written to about 15 others who were in his second tier of choices, thanking them for their interest and time. Tennessee coach Phillip Fulmer was on a recruiting trip and he also was in a hotel. When Peyton called at 6 a.m., it was as if a good dream had awakened him. Fulmer reacted as if he had won the lottery, which in a sense he had, boosting the viability and visibility of his already thriving Volunteer program even more. "Peyton," Fulmer said, "I'd do cartwheels in the street if they'd let me out there in my pajamas."[10]

In the weeks leading up to his January 25, 1994, press conference, the lobbying intensified in several ways. The coaches were somewhat in the background. Passionate fans took up the recruiting challenge, firing off letters to Peyton demanding that his loyalty to Ole Miss show itself. Of course, Peyton had grown up in New Orleans, not Mississippi, and schools like Louisiana State or Tulane were closer to home and hadn't even made his finalist list.

The long-awaited, where-is-Peyton-headed press conference took place at the Hilton in a room jammed with media personnel from the local area and from Mississippi. He told people his decision had "come up orange," the dominant color in Tennessee uniforms.[11] When he visited Knoxville and saw the school's huge Neyland Stadium, Peyton said he just got the vibes that it was the right place for him to play. "Even now I can't say why I liked it so much," Peyton said years later. "I'd never been there, never seen a game in Neyland Stadium." He said there was even an unfriendly ice storm while he visited, with the ice coating the field. "But for some reason, Tennessee felt right."[12]

Sometime later, when he was participating in a book about his family, Peyton said he also chose the Volunteers because they were in a period where they were playing superior football to the Rebels and he didn't want to be seen as a savior to a program. He had also heard Mississippi might be facing NCAA probation that would knock the team off television and eliminate it from playing in bowl games for a period of time. Some writers observed that Peyton "did not want the special treatment that could have come with his playing at Ole Miss. He also realized that the larger, more successful program and passing offense at Tennessee was more suited to transforming him into the best quarterback he could be."[13]

Peyton said when the news conference ended he was glad, though it wasn't terribly taxing, but as soon as knowledge of his decision spread, "all hell broke loose."[14]

Peyton did admit having mixed emotions. The University of Mississippi and its football program had meant a lot to him while he was growing up. Not only did his parents attend the school, but other relatives were alumni, too. His father was still linked to the Rebels and wouldn't have it any other way. So he did suffer a teeny bit of buyer's remorse. "I felt like I was saying no to all my relatives who had gone to school there, and a lot of my friends who were there," Peyton said.[15]

His was an individual choice to play college football at the place where he believed he would best fit. Peyton had nothing against Ole Miss and nothing against Mississippi. He was quite fond of both the school and the state. After careful consideration, he just decided it was not for him. That was the simple answer, but Mississippians did not take no for an answer. There was anger, even fury, that Peyton had selected another SEC school over Mississippi. Hate mail poured in to Isidore Newman School. Hate mail poured into the Mannings' mailbox. Hate phone calls came in on the telephone. It seemed Peyton was guilty of dumping toxic waste in a lake, not merely volunteering to play quarterback for the Volunteers.

People from the southern United States pride themselves on their charm, graciousness, and hospitality. The fan reaction to Peyton's choice may have set those images back a decade or more. Letter writers to the *Jackson Clarion-Ledger* newspaper questioned Peyton's loyalty. Four-letter words were overheard being attached to his name. "Somebody needs to get a whip to that boy," an unknown observer said.[16]

Peyton said that the place his father had always loved, that had shaped him, made him famous, and led him to his wife and career, turned on Archie and that it was a terrible thing to see. He called some of the phone calls to the house "indignant" and "brutal" because he had chosen Tennessee. "And while it hurt me a lot, it hurt mainly because of what it did to my dad. He was devastated. The calls, the letters, the disrespect shown a man who had done so much for that school ... it was cruel." Letters followed phone calls in which Mississippi supporters said they used to love Archie Manning, but no more and said they hoped Peyton got hurt or broke his leg. They said he had made the worst mistake of his life by selecting Tennessee, though it was difficult to see how a vicious campaign like this would make Peyton think so.

Peyton said his father received more than 200 letters "attacking my choice" and that he was told the *Jackson Clarion-Ledger* received 7,000 phone calls on the topic. He briefly worried about Cooper's safety at Ole Miss, but true to his own personality, Cooper took to wearing a Tennessee Volunteer baseball cap around campus.[17]

The bad feeling toward the Mannings lingered for months, Peyton said, and showed up in peculiar ways. Archie and Olivia still made regular trips to Mississippi and not long after Peyton committed to Tennessee, the gas station attendant at the family's regular stop along the highway said they weren't welcome to fill their tank there anymore. Archie was stunned when he realized the fellow was serious.

For a while, there was a schism between Archie Manning and his alma mater, but not for very long. He helped recruit other players for the Rebels, convinced as he had always been that it was a genuinely great place to get an education and play college football. Like a judge with a conflict of interest, however, he had recused himself from his son's case. It was not his position to meddle, he believed strongly, and even in the face of verbal and written abuse he never felt he had made the wrong decision. It should be up to any young man to weigh the information and make the choice where he wants to spend four years of his life.

"I love Ole Miss, but I can't say I love Ole Miss more than my son," Archie Manning said. "I love him more."[18]

It was a voice of common sense, a voice that any fan thinking more clearly might have heeded while thinking about his children. This was one time, however, when the long version of the word "fan" applied to the situation. Although it is rarely spoken aloud in describing spectators at a sporting event, the word stems from "fanatic."

NOTES

1. Archie Manning, Peyton Manning, and John Underwood, *Manning* (New York: HarperEntertainment, 2000), 208.

2. Jimmy Hyams, *Peyton Manning—Primed and Ready* (Lenexa, KS: Addax Publishing Group, 1998), 33.

3. Ibid., 34.

4. Manning, Manning, and Underwood, *Manning,* 232.

5. Hyams, *Peyton Manning,* 34.

6. Manning, Manning, and Underwood, *Manning,* 230.

7. Ibid., 231.

8. Ibid., 235.

9. Ibid.

10. Ibid., 237.

11. Hyams, *Peyton Manning,* 35.

12. Manning, Manning, and Underwood, *Manning,* 234.

13. Tim Polzer, *Peyton Manning: Leader On and Off the Field* (Berkeley Heights, NJ: Enslow Publishing, 2006), 49.

14. Manning, Manning, and Underwood, *Manning,* 237.

15. Hyams, *Peyton Manning,* 35.

16. Ibid., 37.

17. Manning, Manning, and Underwood, *Manning,* 238–39.

18. Hyams, *Peyton Manning,* 38.

Chapter 5

A FRESHMAN STAR IS BORN
AT TENNESSEE

Peyton Manning chose to be a Volunteer and suddenly orange meant more to him than just carving a pumpkin at Halloween. When Tennessee football fans fill Neyland Stadium for a Southeastern Conference game, it's a pretty good bet that most of the 105,000 of them will be decked out in orange garb, t-shirt, jersey, or jacket, depending on the weather. It's a demonstration of allegiance to the players wearing the numbered orange jerseys on the field.

Commitment to Volunteer football dates back about a century and any player who makes it through four years as a member of the team is bound to have an orange-dominated wardrobe. The University of Tennessee Lady Vols, the women's basketball team, has won eight NCAA titles under coach Pat Summitt. While there are other universities in the state, and the Nashville Predators compete in the National Hockey League and the Memphis Grizzlies play in the NBA, no team in the state anywhere from Chattanooga to Memphis can compete for fan allegiance with UT football. Tennessee football is not only the biggest game in town, it is the biggest game for many miles around.

Peyton Manning understood that. If there were any gaps in his UT football education, they were filled in during the recruiting period. That was one of the things he loved about SEC football—that the fans considered it number 1 in their sports rooting lives. There were great football teams all over the country, but Manning's heart lay with the SEC and the South, and in only a few of the cities around the conference did fans have their attention divided during autumn by also supporting a neighborhood NFL team. If you were a Florida Gator supporter, you might well be a Jacksonville Jaguar backer, too. If you were a Georgia Bulldog rooter, you might well be an Atlanta Falcons fan as well. Tennessee fans did not let any pro team interfere with their emotional devotion to the Volunteers.

Some blue-chip recruits who can pick among any of dozens of top programs, especially in basketball, might be looking for a head coach to tell them they will be a starter immediately. Most big-time college football programs have someone waiting in the wings to replace a departing senior, someone who has also been highly sought-after and someone who has more experience, even as a red-shirt just running through opponents' plays for a year. No college football head coach of integrity and honesty will promise an incoming freshman that he will become an instant starter. There are too many variables. Even if the coach believes it to be likely (and most coaches hesitate to believe their good fortune that a true freshman, either still 17 or just turned 18, can show up and start), history indicates showing caution is a wise approach. A returning player can mature over the summer and surprise the coaching staff. The hot-shot recruit can show up for summer camp out of shape or with an injury.

The best course of action is to inform the newcomer that he will be given every consideration and that if all goes well he will get his chance. Peyton Manning knew how things worked. If any coach had made such an unequivocal promise that he would be the starter, Peyton likely would have doubted the coach's honesty and chosen another school. Being given a chance to develop, having a chance to get into a few games, was all that he asked for. Peyton being Peyton, he showed up for Tennessee's preseason camp in prime shape and with a summer's worth of quarterback study crammed into his head. He even enrolled at Tennessee for summer school to get a head start on his college experience.

"I was hoping to play some as a freshman," Manning said. "Coach Fulmer had said I might. I didn't want to red-shirt."[1] A red-shirt year, often taken by players who want to mature mentally and physically as freshmen, would mean he would only be able to practice, not play in any games.

Manning had supreme confidence in his ability, but he knew that Tennessee was set at quarterback. Jerry Colquitt, a fifth-year senior who had waited his entire college career to start as signal-caller, was number 1 on the depth chart. Colquitt was only in the job because the real number 1, Heath Shuler, who would have been a senior, turned pro early, leaving the spot open. The second-stringer was a local sports hero, a junior named Todd Helton. A native of Knoxville, Helton was an all-around athlete who was even more highly regarded as a baseball player, an evaluation that proved correct. Helton eventually became an All-Star .300-plus hitter for the Colorado Rockies. The other quarterbacks on the roster were red-shirt freshman Mike Grein and another true freshman, Branndon Stewart.

Stewart, like Manning, was a highly coveted prospect. From Stephensville, Texas, Stewart was not only a high school superstar football player, but he also had tremendous physical strength as a weightlifter and was a first-rate high jumper. Fulmer had signed two of the country's hottest incoming freshman quarterbacks, both rated in the top 10 at the position. It certainly provided long-term insurance for the Vols, but it also seemed destined to create a logjam at a position where only one man could take the field at a time.

Before even arriving in Knoxville, Manning took advantage of an invitation to take throwing practice with the New Orleans Saints as they gathered for their pre-NFL workouts. Pat Swilling, one of the team's toughest defenders, told reporters that it looked as if Manning was ready for the pro league right then and there.[2] Although he was invited to participate in Louisiana's summer football high school all-star game, Manning decided to skip it so he could concentrate on his summer classes at UT and fully prepare his game for the next level.

Long a student of the game who took advantage of every opportunity to increase his knowledge about playing quarterback, Manning did more than dabble in a few summer courses. He also spent much of his free time in the Tennessee film room reviewing the team's performance in selected games. He was simultaneously taking two courses of study, a double major so to speak. "If I was not in class, I was doing something to make myself a better football player," Manning said. Manning spent so much time hunkered down in a dark room that his teammates began calling him "Caveman."[3] Whether those players who were trying to enjoy their summer vacation recognized it or not, this work ethic, this time spent absorbing football, was what set Manning apart from most other players they teamed with or knew. If he had to sacrifice sunshine, swimming, fishing, or pickup basketball time in order to improve his game, he didn't hesitate. Anyone who might have believed that Archie Manning was pushing his son all of the time at home would have to acknowledge this body of evidence—it was Peyton who was the motivator.

Word got to the reporters who covered Tennessee football that Manning was a workaholic and one of them wrote a glib line that was right on the money. "Manning watched more film than Siskel and Ebert," the sports writer penned.[4]

For weeks, Manning continued his full-court press of learning the offense and trying to cram years worth of Tennessee on-field history into his head. He developed the slick trick of leaving the door to the film room open a sliver so that any coach passing by would realize he was in there studying. Manning wanted to learn, but he also wanted the coaches to take note of his efforts. In group quarterback meetings with offensive coordinator David Cutcliffe, Manning, like a contestant on a quiz show hitting the buzzer first, would sometimes answer questions that weren't even directed his way. He wanted to show off his knowledge. Cutcliffe and Helton both began calling him "R2D2" after the robot in the *Star Wars* movies that appeared to be a know-it-all and Helton expressed resentment when Manning cut him off.[5]

There was not the slightest hint that Manning could move up the depth chart his freshman year to become the starting quarterback for the Vols. There was only the vaguest suggestion that he might have an opportunity to take a snap from center all season. The crowd in front of him on the team depth chart was too thick. Colquitt had waited his turn and it was now his time. Helton had a lock on the backup job. Grein quit the team, leaving four quarterbacks. If you are the third-best starting pitcher in the rotation, you will throw regularly. If you are the third- (or fourth-) rated quarterback on a football team, the odds are very high against your getting grass stains on your uniform on any given Saturday and maybe not even once all year.

Yet just as there are miracle plays that turn around the results in games, the history of the personnel on sports teams tells some remarkable, unexpected tales. Usually, when a starter goes down with an injury, there is a falloff in performance at his position. That is to be expected given that the hurt player was number 1 and the backup number 2. Sometimes a team weathers the psychological blow and rallies together behind the backup to play better than ever. And sometimes someone situated father down the depth chart emerges and becomes the legitimate number 1 starter, surprising everyone from coaches to players to fans, even himself.

Tennessee opened its 1994 football season at UCLA in the Rose Bowl. It was not one of the heavenly stadiums of the SEC that Peyton had been weaned on, but as host of the annual Rose Bowl game it was one of the most storied football arenas in the country. Manning said he talked to his grandfather, Cooper Williams, on the telephone before the game and he urged Peyton to stay ready because "I bet you'll play."

Manning did all he could not to burst out laughing, and informed Grandpa that there was no way he would get into the game, in fact actually employing the phrase, "No way in the world."[6] Archie and Olivia did make the trip west to attend the game even though they had no expectations Peyton would actually see action.

As scheduled, Colquitt started at quarterback. However, on the seventh play of Tennessee's possession, while running an option play, Colquitt tore an anterior cruciate ligament (ACL) in his knee. The injury immediately ruined his season. Helton, the next man up, took over the offense. For the next three series of downs, Helton was in charge, trying to jump-start a slow-starting offense that couldn't dent the Bruins' defense. Fulmer and offensive coordinator David Cutcliffe decided to shake things up.

Coach Fulmer gave Manning the word: "Get your arm loose!" he shouted on the sidelines against the backdrop din of the crowd.[7]

Curious about the hubbub of activity on the Tennessee sideline, an ABC television camera showed freshman Peyton Manning starting to warm up. Legendary college football broadcaster Keith Jackson drank in the scene and situation in seconds and told the audience, "There's one pair of sweaty palms right there."[8]

This was the moment Peyton Manning had dreamed about his entire life. He had planned for it, studied for it, and arguably was the most poised and mature freshman quarterback in the country. But Jackson was correct. Manning was as nervous as if he was asking a girl out on a date for the first time (and yes, he had done so, in between practicing football). Manning thought he would be ready for the moment when the call came, but even he later admitted he was not really prepared, if only because the moment out of the blue. "I was shaking," he said. "My heart started pounding." And then the coaches uttered the phrase that launched Manning's college football career: "'You're going in.' I'll never forget those words."[9] Later, Peyton couldn't help but marvel about his grandfather's intuition. Cooper Williams was probably the only human in the nation who foresaw any possibility of his grandson getting into the UCLA game.

This did not mean that Manning had beaten out Stewart in their personal duel to become Tennessee's quarterback of the future because Fulmer also told Stewart to stay ready, that he was going to play that day, too. As time passed and the changing of the quarterback became permanent at Tennessee, those outside the program took it for granted that Manning and Stewart had a heated rivalry and that they were actually enemies. Manning said that was not the case, that they were friendly. However, they were highly competitive and the two occasionally took advantage of small opportunities to demonstrate one-upmanship. Knowing that Stewart was a powerful weightlifter pushed Manning to lift more and more weight in order to keep up. Stewart once asked Manning if he wanted to watch film together. Manning said no and then spent two hours watching film himself in order to gain an edge. On a day when the building where the football team met was locked, Manning kicked aside the block holding open the outside door so Stewart would be late. He admitted later he had been "sneaky," but said he thought Stewart was so good he had to do any little thing to catch up and gain an advantage.[10]

Volunteer fans had been primed for a one-year Colquitt era, confident that the seasoned senior could lead the team. They were glad Fulmer had nabbed two prized freshman quarterbacks, but they neither expected nor wanted them to play a significant role running the team anytime soon. The track record of freshmen quarterbacks at big-time programs did not engender confidence. A learning curve was always expected.

"When Colquitt went down, Vol Network broadcaster Bill Anderson hit the bottom of the broadcast table, bemoaning the loss of the senior signal-caller," wrote one university employee later, "a scene which was repeated across Big Orange Country. What was a broken dream for Colquitt became a great opportunity for Manning, though no one outside the Vol family really knew it at the time."[11]

Up in the stands, Olivia Manning noticed that Peyton was warming up and informed her husband that he was going into the game. Archie immediately replied that Peyton wasn't going in. He was wrong.[12]

Whether they read the nervousness on his face, in his tone of voice, or in the blather that streamed from his mouth when he reached the huddle and shouted, "All right, guys, here we go!" as if he had been running the UT offense his entire life, Peyton got a brief comeuppance when tackle Jason Layman, who like the other upperclassmen might well have wondered what the heck was going on that day with quarterback ins and outs, said, "Just shut the f—up and call the play!" Not responding aloud, the words running through Manning's mind were, "Well, OK, I could do that."[13]

Fantasyland had gone about as far as it would for the moment. Manning did not immediately throw a long touchdown pass to rally his team. In his first series at the helm of the UT offense he handed the ball off to running backs three straight times. When the Vols did not gain a first down he jogged back off the field so his team could punt.

That was Manning's only turn at running the team that day. Stewart also got a chance, but Fulmer went back to Helton after a little while and Helton engineered a comeback that fell just short. Mostly, after the loss, there was mourning on behalf of Colquitt, who never played again for Tennessee, but there was considerable hullabaloo about the freshmen getting into the game. Nobody really attached tremendous importance to it, though, because Helton had moved up to become the number 1 quarterback and he had much more experience.

For the moment, there was no starting quarterback controversy. If anything, the competition between Manning and Stewart ratcheted up for the chance to gain solid footing as the backup. There are times when the second-stringer at quarterback on a football team can be as forgotten as the vice president. But other times the job of a second-stringer might mean action in every game and they knew that.

Tennessee had a solid all-around team and star running back James Stewart was heavily relied upon to move the first-down chains and score touchdowns. Helton managed the offense well and threw to his cadre of wide receivers to keep things in balance. He was comfortable running the show, but Tennessee's results were mixed. There was an impressive 41-23 win over Georgia, but a harrowing 31-0 loss to Florida. At various times Fulmer inserted Manning and Stewart into the games to run a few series. They absorbed the scene, got used to playing in front of 100,000 people, and completed their first collegiate passes. But Tennessee was only 1-3, a record that was nearly poor enough to send Volunteer fans from Beale Street to Smoky Mountain National Park into heart palpitations.

In the season's fourth game, Helton hurt a knee. It was not as severe an injury as Colquitt's, but going into the next game, against Washington State, at the time ranked number 1 in the nation in defense, Tennessee had to count on two freshman quarterbacks. Throughout the preseason and early season Manning had shown many signs that he felt he was ready to take over and run Tennessee's offense, even if he knew his place. But now he was being handed the chance to start, much more quickly than he expected.

Prior to the game against the Cougars, Fulmer took Manning aside for a chat. Fully comprehending what a big moment it was for his young quarterback, and also understanding the skills that made Manning unique, Fulmer still wanted to keep his hands on the reins. He wanted to quell any desires Manning might have to run wild with the offense. He told him to "play conservatively" and "avoid interceptions." It was not a full vote of confidence, but Manning understood he was in the game on a trial basis and it was only others' misfortune and happenstance that had put him on the firing line so early in his UT career. He wanted to take advantage, but he didn't want to irritate the head coach and be benched. This would not be a passing festival. Manning ended up attempting just 14 passes and completing 7 of them. He did not have the run of the playbook, but he did nothing to discourage his future availability. For the moment, only just for the moment, it was enough for the impatient Peyton.[14]

Helton eventually devoted all of his focus to baseball and has produced what might be a Hall of Fame career. Manning started his first game. There were no breathers on the schedule. Manning had fantasized about playing his college career in the SEC, and here was the SEC in his face, full force, one week Alabama, the next week Arkansas. There were no gimmes. Fulmer continued to use Manning and Stewart judiciously and each young talent had his notable moments.

The victory over Arkansas on October 8, 1994, was a milestone. Tennessee won the game, 38-21, and it was Manning's first win as a Volunteer starting quarterback. Manning's final numbers paled next to the statistics he would record in the coming years, but he completed 12 out of 19 attempts for two touchdown passes.

When the regular season ended, Tennessee's record was 7-4 and Manning had established his position in the pecking order. It was apparent that he was the number 1 quarterback and the Vols' quarterback of the future. The Volunteers received an invitation to meet Virginia Tech in the Gator Bowl. On December 30 Manning led UT to a 45-23 win in the bowl. It was a satisfying end to a surprising first season in Knoxville. Manning was named the SEC Freshman of the Year. He completed 89 out of 144 pass attempts for a completion rate of 61.8 percent and 1,141 yards.

The war for the starting quarterback job had not been confined to an in-house debate. At Tennessee's level of college football, major personnel changes like that are fair-game topics in the newspapers. Beyond that, fans who paid for season tickets or merely rooted from their own living rooms always made their opinions known. If either Manning or Stewart had a bad stretch during a game, the booing might well start up at Neyland Stadium. It didn't matter that the quarterbacks were members of the home team; whichever one of them was on the sideline looked better to the paying customers at the moment if the incumbent was having an off-day, or an off-series. Manning ended up having more good series than Stewart and that's why he became the number 1 quarterback.

Stewart had fallen victim to Manning's exceptional preparation and to his blossoming talent. Given that Manning emerged to become one of the greatest quarterbacks in the history of the sport, his ascension was likely only a matter of time. However, Stewart's parents were very unhappy about their son's relegation to second-string. They felt he was being treated unfairly and that Manning was no better than he was. At one point after a game, Stewart's mother pounded on the door of the Volunteer locker room, convinced that Archie Manning was inside procuring special treatment for his son. The father was nowhere near the locker room at the time.

Peyton said that Archie—just as he had when his sons had played high school ball—took pains to stay away from the daily operations of Tennessee football. In fact, he skipped one of Peyton's games that season in order to be in attendance at one of Eli's junior high games because of a conflict in scheduling. "Dad always kept a respectful distance on those things [the playbook and playing time]," Peyton said. "I mean, he didn't even want to know our plays or what the thinking was about them."[15]

During the off-season Stewart transferred to Texas A&M where he found success quarterbacking the Aggies.

Early in his college career, Manning did develop a special bond with David Cutcliffe, the Volunteers' offensive coordinator, who was the beneficiary of the young man's study habits and growth into an All-American quarterback. Over time the men became very close friends, though at the beginning, Cutcliffe was as curious as anyone how the Manning-Stewart competition would play out.

"Truth be known, Peyton was much more prepared to play," Cutcliffe said. "Branndon was a good football player, but we were probably more unfair to Peyton. Peyton was more prepared to play. Peyton knew that. Jerry Colquitt knew that. Todd Helton knew that. Sure, Branndon knew that, too. He didn't know half of what Peyton knew. Peyton outworked Branndon. But Branndon's mother knew more about coaching than I did."[16]

It didn't take very long watching Manning throw passes and run the offense for the upperclassmen in the huddle to show their respect for him. No one else told him to shut up and just call the play that season. "He came in with an attitude I'd never seen before," said Eric Lane, one of the Tennessee players, reflecting on how hard Manning worked to be ready when his chance arose as a freshman.[17]

By the end of his freshman season, after getting the chance to play regularly, and succeeding when he did so, Manning had gained nationwide attention from people who really knew the game. Bill Walsh, the former coach of the San Francisco 49ers, who had been credited with perfecting the "West Coast Offense" that was all the rage, marveled at Manning's ability at a young age. "He's further along than any college quarterback I've seen in years," said the Super Bowl–winning coach who mentored Joe Montana in the pros. "Maybe ever."[18]

On most football teams, from the top tier of NCAA play to the NFL, the head coach is more of a CEO than a day-to-day coach of individual players. There might be 100 young men on a college team and their roles are broken down by position. Their position coach is the guy with whom they deal most often and who most closely supervises their drills. Manning and Cutcliffe grew into close pals, not only pupil and coach, but genuine friends. As his years passed at Tennessee, Manning dined at Cutcliffe's house and played with his children. They thought alike and respected each other's knowledge.

Archie Manning had always tutored his son in a general way, providing information about the sport of football and always answering his questions. But when he sent him off to college he more or less told him to just work hard and listen to his coaches. He did not send a personal family Manning playbook along. He did not presume to intrude on what the team and its coaches planned. He stepped back. He and Peyton spoke often, but frequently what Peyton had to talk about transcended football. He had met a girl, Ashley, during his summer school period, and they ended up dating throughout his career. (They married in 2001.) Peyton told Archie about Ashley. He told him about the campus. He told him that he was worried about the competition from Branndon Stewart. But Archie wasn't his coach and was never involved in the intricacies of improving his form. Peyton picked up his cues from game film and from Cutcliffe.

In June of 1994, several months after Peyton agreed to attend Tennessee, and the month before he was planning to move on campus, Cutcliffe made a pilgrimage to the Manning home in New Orleans to review the UT offense. He asked Archie to be present, but Peyton said Archie fell asleep in his chair a half an hour after the discussions began.

"It was his way of saying, 'I don't care about your plays. I don't want to know about them,'" Peyton said. "'You coach my son and I'll be there for the other things.' I admit it was harder when dad first said, 'You do what you think is best and I'll support you.' But it was his way of giving me my rite of passage."[19]

As a freshman arriving in Knoxville during that summer, Peyton Manning had been one of a quintet of contenders for the quarterback job. Under ordinary circumstances he would never have had the chance to start eight games for the Volunteers during his first season. But what his coaches and all of Tennessee football fandom realized as the leaves changed colors that autumn was that they were witnessing emerging greatness.

When Manning returned to campus in the fall of 1995 for his sophomore season, there would be no quarterback debate, no quarterback controversy. Manning was The Man now.

NOTES

1. Archie Manning, Peyton Manning, and John Underwood, *Manning* (New York: HarperEntertainment, 2000), 242.

2. Jimmy Hyams, *Peyton Manning—Primed and Ready* (Lenexa, KS: Addax Publishing Group, 1998), 80.

3. Manning, Manning, and Underwood, *Manning*, 242.

4. Tom Mattingly, *Tennessee Football—The Peyton Manning Years* (Charlotte, NC: UMI Publications, 1998), 55.

5. Hyams, *Peyton Manning*, 83.

6. Manning, Manning, and Underwood, *Manning*, 249.

7. Hyams, *Peyton Manning*, 78.

8. Ibid., 78.

9. Ibid.

10. Manning, Manning, and Underwood, *Manning*, 244–45.

11. Mattingly, *Tennessee Football*, 56.

12. Manning, Manning, and Underwood, *Manning*, 250.

13. Ibid., 251.

14. Tim Polzer, *Peyton Manning: Leader On and Off the Field* (Berkeley Heights, NJ: Enslow Publishers, 2006), 52–53.

15. Manning, Manning, and Underwood, *Manning*, 247.

16. Hyams, *Peyton Manning*, 89.

17. Mark Stewart, *Peyton Manning—Rising Son* (Brookfield, CT: Millbrook Press, 2000), 12.

18. Ibid., 16.

19. Manning, Manning, and Underwood, *Manning*, 247–48.

Chapter 6

EVERYBODY'S ALL-AMERICAN

Peyton Manning was the undisputed first-string quarterback at the University of Tennessee in the fall of 1995, his sophomore year. It was almost as if Manning had participated in a Tough Man boxing contest and defeated all comers. Any quarterback who was still wearing orange knew from preseason summer camp on that his main job was likely to be wearing headphones communicating with the coaches in the press box upstairs at Neyland Stadium, not running plays on the field.

Supervising plays was Peyton Manning's full-time job and the only way any other quarterback was going to wrestle the pigskin away from him was if Coach Phillip Fulmer felt a game was hopelessly lost or overwhelmingly in the team's possession. In other words, it would take a scoreboard slaughter for Manning to be rested.

If freshman year was Manning's coming-out party, his sophomore year was his coronation, as he exploded on the national scene at the helm of the Volunteer offense. Manning had achieved one goal by becoming the starting quarterback of an SEC football team. But very true to his character, he did not take it easy once he established that he was capable in that role. He worked just as hard, watched just as much film, did drill after drill with the goal of improving.

The most surprising aspect of Manning's focus was the way he was able to step back and evaluate his own style and form. Despite his early success, between his freshman and sophomore seasons, Manning decided that his passing form needed tweaking. It would have been easy, even logical, to stick with what had been working for several years, but Manning felt he could improve more if he overhauled his throwing approach. So Manning went to work on the repetition required to alter his natural and ingrained motion with the goal of improving his passing mechanics and adopting a higher release point for his passes. Such a change requires endless repetition and was a drastic move reminiscent of Tiger Woods overhauling his stroke at the top of his game.

"He never wanted to stop getting better," Tennessee offensive coordinator David Cutcliffe said."[1]

Indeed, there was the risk that too much tinkering would leave Manning out of synch and throw off the smoothness of his delivery. More than quarterbacks, top-flight pitchers grapple with these types of changes to their pitching motion. They can pay for their changes by getting hammered by a string of batters. For Manning, surrendering a form that had proven reliable in exchange for the unknown, which might pay dividends, took fortitude. There was a potential downside. What if he was not as accurate throwing with the quicker release? There was only one way to find out.

Manning might well have been equally as effective a quarterback his sophomore year if he had made no changes. Chances are that experience alone would have made him better. But he chose to break down his form and take on the challenge of reinventing himself based on the possibility that he would get better. "I figured with guys blitzing and coming at you, I needed a quicker release," Manning said.[2] Defenders in college football were bigger, stronger, and faster than they were when Manning played high school ball in Louisiana and it went without saying that the same would prove true when he moved on to the NFL. Manning chose to adapt when the easy thing to do would have been to stand pat.

Manning unveiled his new form in the season opener against East Carolina and things went smoothly. He was just as sharp as he had been and he passed the test. From then on Manning was a slightly improved model of Manning the freshman. The casual fan might never have noticed, but quarterback experts could see a difference in his game.

"You'd think he was a walk-on trying to prove something," said Tennessee's strength and conditioning coach of Manning's hard work. "He's really a driven young man."[3]

By circumstance, the team leader, or at least one of the team leaders, is the quarterback. He signals the plays, he directs the offense, and the ball is in his hands. Demeanor counts, too. Unlike Manning's cameo appearance in his first game as a freshman, he knew that the only voice in the huddle should be his own. After the UT quarterback shuffle, Manning was the last man standing and there was no doubt in the Volunteers' minds about who was in charge. A football player can gain respect from his teammates in various ways. Sometimes pure athletic ability will do it. Other times a knack for rescuing the team when its back is against the wall can be a source of admiration. Hard work is another. Obvious support from the coaches that this guy is the extension of them on the field also sends a message. Manning had all of that going for him. The other Volunteers in the lineup knew Manning outworked just about everyone. They knew that their coaches believed in him, and that he knew his stuff on the field. Unfettered by competition from other quarterbacks and given more freedom to use his throwing gifts, Manning became a full-fledged star as a sophomore.

He set a school record throwing for 2,954 yards and he tossed 22 touchdown passes. With Manning, the Volunteers became far more pass-oriented than they had been. He attempted 380 passes during the season, with 64.2 percent completion, and went 132 straight attempts without throwing an interception. The Volunteers had everyone in Tennessee thinking orange en route to an 11-1 season that included a win over Ohio State in the Citrus Bowl, and a final national ranking of number 2. Tennessee football had always been on the map, but it claimed a slightly larger piece of real estate once Manning took control. In a normal college football season, not many sophomores attracted more than minimal attention in the Heisman Trophy voting designating the sport's best player, but Manning finished sixth in the balloting. There really was only one down week in the entire season. The Volunteers were obliterated by SEC rival Florida. By most measurements, Manning was superb that day, throwing for more than 300 yards without an interception, plus two touchdowns, and twice Tennessee led the Gators by 16 points. Yet with a discouraging avalanche of second-half points, Florida buried UT 62-37.

From the hindsight of several years gone by even the sting of the Florida defeat abated somewhat and Manning said the year was very satisfying. "It was one of those years you brag to your grandchildren about and they look at you like they know you're lying," Manning said.[4] Of course, considering what he achieved in the next two years and in his professional career, Manning's sophomore season really might someday be regarded as run-of-the-mill. It certainly felt good, though, maybe feeling better given that it was Manning's first complete college season as the designated first-stringer.

One of Manning's favorite games that season was a 30-27 win over Georgia. It was a home game in Knoxville and it took all of the Volunteers' weapons to outlast the Bulldogs. Manning completed 26 of 38 passes for 349 yards and two touchdowns. There is no elixir like winning and whether a player has a good day on the field or a mediocre one, winning the game is supposed to be the cure-all. But human nature being what it is, a player is going to feel better yet, and feel more like partying and celebrating victory, if his performance was a major reason why the game went into the record books as a "W." On this day, Manning was one of those contributors. "My coming out party," he called it. "I felt like I really helped the team win, whereas other times I just did my part and tried not to get the team beat."[5]

One of the yardsticks used to grade quarterbacks, and one of the things that separates good quarterbacks from great quarterbacks and Hall of Famers, is their ability to win games for their teams. In discussions of great quarterbacks, one area often mentioned is how many times a John Elway, Joe Montana, or Johnny Unitas led fourth-quarter comebacks. Opposing teams trying to hold on to victory were expected to quake in their shoes when they gave the ball back to one of those greats with a couple of minutes remaining on the clock. The phrase "No lead is safe" was applied to those players as long as they had some time to work with. While at Tennessee, Manning aspired to be thought of in the same manner. It was the exact equivalent of the vampire theory, that Dracula would keep coming back to haunt you until you thrust a stake into his heart.

Although the Georgia triumph provided special satisfaction to Manning, another game his sophomore year might have been even better. Playing against Arkansas when the Razorbacks featured the number 1–ranked defense in the league, Manning proved to be the Hogs' ruination, completing 35 passes in 46 attempts for 384 yards and four touchdowns. Although they were trailing 24-14 at one point, the passing game propelled Tennessee to a 49-31 victory.

There was some bad blood between Tennessee and Arkansas at the time. Two years earlier, Arkansas coach Danny Ford was overheard on television saying "I hope he tears up a knee" about UT starting quarterback Heath Shuler. That did not rate highly on the sportsmanship meter and although Shuler was long gone to the pros, when Arkansas defenders blitzed Manning hot and heavy and got in a lick from behind that he didn't think was within the bounds of propriety, Manning ignited a verbal dispute with a Razorback. The verbal fire was Manning's way of fighting back and later he said, "I gave him a little lip service and let him know I didn't like it one bit." Cutcliffe noted dryly, "Arkansas got on the wrong side of Peyton." And he pretty much left them face-down in a ditch.[6]

Cutcliffe was turning into Peyton's biggest fan that was not named Manning. The coach and pupil saw the football world in a like-minded way. "We developed something all quarterbacks and offensive quarterbacks need to have—total communication, available around the clock," Manning said. "With Coach Cut I had a mix of coach and friend. We didn't just talk about football. We talked about life."[7]

Being on the same page as an offensive coordinator is critical for a quarterback, but it is equally as important to be tight with the guys who catch the ball. Pass routes, where the ball is thrown, what each receiver is capable of, who has the best hands, who can jump the highest, all affect whether or not a pass is completed. Oftentimes a quarterback and one receiver develop a near-telepathic ability to understand each other's football thoughts. Success in the passing game can often rely on this special bond. Joe Montana had Jerry Rice. Y.A. Tittle had Del Shofner. There are many such memorable combinations in NFL history. When Manning was at Isidore Newman, his brother Cooper played that role. During his sophomore year at UT, Manning's go-to guy became Joey Kent.

When he was reviewing receiver qualities with Cutcliffe one day, Manning said Kent was the one guy who stood out for his ability to go and get the ball in a crowd. That instinct distinguished Kent's play and Manning's instinct that Kent could be a key player in the passing game was correct. It wasn't as if Manning ignored other receivers who were open to throw to Kent, but Kent was open more frequently than the others. In 1995 Kent caught 69 passes. In 1996 he caught 68. There wasn't the same emotional charge as if Peyton had been throwing to Cooper as a duo in college, but he and Kent cemented a valuable partnership. Once again, the Georgia game sophomore year was the pivotal moment. Kent had said to Manning, "Get me involved." Manning said Kent didn't complain loudly or make a big deal, but on the next possession Manning completed three passes to his receiver and said, "Is that involved enough for you?" As Humphrey Bogart said to his favorite French inspector at the end of *Casablanca*, "Louis, I think this is the beginning of a beautiful friendship." It was.[8]

Once Peyton emerged as the quarterback for Tennessee, there were plenty of media mentions of his father and how the son was following in the dad's footsteps as a college player. Yet those were likely a fraction of such mentions compared to the sensory assault if Peyton had chosen the University of Mississippi. With Peyton playing for the Volunteers, it was more by-the-way discussion than head-to-head comparison. During his recruitment, Ole Miss had pledged to take Archie's retired number 18 jersey out of mothballs and let Peyton wear it, too. At Tennessee Peyton's orange jersey featured number 16 in white numbering. If choosing Tennessee over the Rebels had not made his independent thinking clear and his desire to establish a separate identity, the choice of number solidified it. There was no Archie Manning legacy in Knoxville other than the knowledge that he had once been a fine SEC football player.

In the beginning, given the highly charged reaction to Peyton's decision to play at Tennessee, some of the history colored sportswriters' questions. But when Peyton filled out his athletic department personal background form at UT he made an effort to reinforce the choice. To the standard question of why he chose to attend Tennessee, Peyton wrote, "Because I wanted to go there."[9] It was a pretty simple answer, but anyone who read it and knew the Mannings' situation realized Peyton's choice of Tennessee was far from simple.

The hallmark of Peyton Manning's quarterbacking career, almost from its inception in high school, is that he was preternaturally mature, better prepared, more advanced, and more talented than others his age. That was true throughout high school and his freshman year in college. Now he was going to be measured against college players of all ages, sophomores, juniors, and seniors. That was the new challenge and he met it as a sophomore. His next goal was to be recognized as one of the best quarterbacks in the country.

There was a lot to live up to given the glorious history of Tennessee football. It was not as if the Volunteers had never had superstars in their lineup before and never sent stars along to the pros. Peyton Manning was only the latest of potential greats to play in Knoxville. While Isidore Newman had little tradition in football when the Manning brothers played there, Tennessee's program wished to maintain its excellence. Fulmer, Cutcliffe, and the others were not asking Manning to blaze a path to new territory. Tennessee was a member of the national elite.

The fact that Tennessee had a long and revered tradition is one of the things that attracted Manning to the program. As with the other SEC schools, families had worshipped at the altar of Volunteer football for generations. True orange fans could recite great accomplishments of the past without consulting record books. Devotees could rattle off the names of previous stars and All-Americans. There was a reason that

100,000-plus fans filled Neyland Stadium for home games. They had been entertained for years and they had believed in and supported a winner for years. Volunteer football was part of the fabric of people's lives in and around Knoxville and throughout the state of Tennessee.

The University of Tennessee had had a football team since 1891. The team was not especially successful or regarded as anything very special until the 1920s. Neyland Stadium was constructed in 1921 and the orange-colored jerseys that became such an identifiable part of Tennessee football mystique were first donned in 1922. Although there is a much greater awareness and more social misgiving about public drinking now, the first icon of a rivalry was introduced in 1925 when "the Beer Barrel" became the symbol of the Tennessee-Kentucky rivalry, with the winner gaining possession for a year. Bob Neyland became coach in 1926 and the Volunteers won the SEC title in 1927. Tennessee played in its first bowl game in 1931. The 1939 team shut out all 10 opponents, a stupefying achievement that led a university employee to write, "Were these guys good on defense, or what?"[10]

The Tennessee walking horse became a mascot of sorts, parading onto the field at each home game and becoming part of football culture. During three different tenures (interrupted by military service) Neyland commanded the football troops. In 1951 a Neyland-coached squad won the Volunteers' first national championship. The venerable coach retired after the next season.

Throughout the years, Tennessee fans exulted when players such as Johnny Majors, Doug Atkins, Conredge Holloway, Richmond Flowers, Reggie White, Steve DeLong, and Heath Shuler performed great exploits on both sides of the ball, and they sang along by the hundreds of thousands as "Rocky Top" took root as a school theme song. As Peyton Manning well knew from his research while being recruited, Tennessee was bursting with tradition. This is precisely the type of southern football lore he wanted to become part of and to leave his mark on. Manning never specifically stated that he wanted to make Tennessee fans forget all of the other Volunteer heroes, but his performances threatened to eclipse all of those that came before him.

Fans of college football programs like Tennessee's are very demanding, hard on coaches, and intolerant of what they deem to be failure. While a record of 7-4 might be cause for celebration at a school with lesser expectations playing in a league like the Mid-American Conference (MAC), mentally it might be considered closer to 4-7 at an SEC power. Supporters, who may donate extravagant amounts of money to their favorite university for library fundraising and stadium renovation, as well as paying top dollar for prime game tickets, begin each season hoping for an undefeated campaign and a shot at the national championship. They can be satisfied with a 10-win season, a league title, and a bowl game. Any achievements that fall under that level raise eyebrows and provoke at least some grumbling. No one ever said that viewpoint was fair, or particularly healthy, but the ante had been raised in college football with the phenomenal amounts of money at stake from television rights and payouts from the top tier of bowl games. Playing in one of the big four games—the Rose Bowl, Fiesta Bowl, Orange Bowl, or Sugar Bowl—might mean a bonanza of $13 million.

The same fans had long memories. To them, a victory over a certain school might be more meaningful than a win over another team. To them, a loss to a certain school might also be more difficult to swallow. By Manning's sophomore year at Tennessee, the Volunteers were in a nine-year slump against Alabama (the best the Vols could muster in that time period was one tie). This truly galled Tennessee backers. They couldn't stand that the Crimson Tide's bragging rights seemed to date back to when Bear Bryant was still living. Manning said that when he first got to campus some fans told him, "Peyton, just beat Alabama for us. We don't care if you go 1-10 as long as you beat Alabama."[11] Of course, that was more a demonstration of emotion than literally true, because if the Vols finished 1-10, those fans would have tarred and feathered Fulmer and thrown Manning's suitcase into the street right behind him as they ran the coach out of town.

In 1995 Tennessee was 5-1, its confidence growing by the minute, when the Alabama game rolled around on the schedule. Sick of losing and being the underdog, Tennessee coaches drew up a bold game plan. On the Vols' first play from scrimmage, Manning threw deep, hit a running Joey Kent in stride, and rang up an 80-yard touchdown to set the tone. Later, Manning had his number called. This almost never happened. Manning was not a swift runner, as he readily admitted, and he was not a running quarterback in the sense that plays were not put into the game plan for him to run as opposed to handing off or throwing. This time an assistant coach called for a fake handoff. Manning did not tell his teammates, and when the ball was hiked Manning tucked the football under his arm and ran around end completely ignored. The fake was so convincing that an official signaled that the touchdown was good by a Tennessee running back who didn't even have the ball. Manning was so open on his jog into the end zone he could have out-cantered the Tennessee walking horse.

Tennessee prevailed, 41-14, that day, and Manning said, "It was party the whole night." The players, Manning included, lit up and inhaled victory cigars, filling their locker room with dense tobacco smoke. "It was more than just a win on a Saturday night," Manning said. "It meant a lot."[12]

Life at Tennessee was going swimmingly. Manning worked hard at his classes and his game. He was expanding his reputation with each victory and he was happy dating Ashley, the girl he met during his weeks at summer school. He stayed in close touch with his family and his father attended every game. Brother Cooper was Peyton's biggest cheerleader and supporter and he was the Manning sentinel on the Ole Miss campus. He saw Peyton play when he could make it to games. Cooper had developed an interest in sports broadcasting and for a brief period thought it might be a career option. During Tennessee's game against Kentucky, Cooper finagled a press pass for a TV station working as a sideline reporter. This was one time Peyton did not know his sibling would be at the game.

Early in the game, Peyton threw an interception. Cooper, who apparently felt that it was his responsibility to inform his younger brother just how bad the pass looked, appeared on the sideline next to number 16 and let him have it, yelling, "What kind of play was that? What were you thinking?"

Peyton was stunned to see his brother at the game, amazed to have him shouting at him, and rather ticked off about having his game focus interrupted. "What are you doing here?" Peyton yelled back. "Get out of here! I'll call security and have you thrown out of here." Cooper went back to keeping track of injuries for the broadcast and Peyton went back to winning the game.[13]

The first full season under Manning's guidance led Tennessee to the Citrus Bowl. Holiday college football games, the majority contested over Christmas vacation, are a reward for a solid winning season. The better the season, the more prestigious the bowl and the Citrus Bowl was a middle-tier bowl. After semester finals, the Volunteers were able to travel to Florida and get in some sightseeing and play time. During a visit to Universal Studios, Manning posed for a photograph with a Bullwinkle the Moose imitator. Manning has a long neck and standing side by side with the mascot-type character provided his teammates with teasing fodder. They slapped the nickname "Bullwinkle" on him. Manning retaliated by issuing a running patter imitating each of his receivers, making fun of how they would each return to the huddle claiming to be open on every play.[14]

The win over Ohio State, while other highly rated teams were losing, fixed Tennessee at number 2 in the season-ending poll. With Manning returning along with a host of other talented players, the first mentions of Tennessee as a national championship contender spilled into print in season wrap-ups.

For his part, Archie Manning, as he had planned all along, receded more into the background than during the recruiting period, and stayed busy as a fan. It took some time, over a year, before the bruised feelings of Mississippi adherents were assuaged. The Mannings had a listed phone number and Archie regularly received phone calls denouncing him for allowing Peyton to go to Tennessee. Despite the rudeness of many of the unhappy Ole Miss fans, Manning heard them out and did not give them the satisfaction of responding with nastiness. He said no friendships among true friends were lost. He also recognized what was at work—a blind support of the fans' favorite team.

"What needs to be understood about college fans," he said, "especially at those state school strongholds where the game is so big, is that for many of them the scoreboard on Saturday afternoon is the centerpiece of their lives, the affirmation of their 'faith' in football. They get so wrapped up in the team that nothing in their life is more important than winning. Whole lifetimes revolve around it. I love that allegiance to a large extent, but when it gets out of proportion to other priorities, it can turn ugly. Anywhere."[15]

All of his meticulous research related to choosing a school aside, one thing Peyton did not look into when he was selecting Tennessee was its future schedule. Coach Fulmer told Peyton that the Volunteers weren't even scheduled to play Mississippi during Manning's four years. He lied. The Rebels were down on the schedule for Manning's junior and senior years. The first one was being played in Oxford.

At the end of Peyton's sophomore year he wanted to rev up his teammates and get in some summertime workouts in preparation for the next season. Once spring practice is over, under NCAA rules coaches cannot call practices or work with their players in formal drills. Manning the workaholic went around putting up signs in athletic buildings and dorms to get the message across to his teammates that he expected them to turn out for extra workouts with him. One sign read, "Throwing at 5:30, Seven-on-Seven." Another read, "One-on-One Drills, 5:30 Wednesday. Mandatory!" Nice work ethic, but the coaches followed Manning around ripping down the signs because it was against the rules to conduct mandatory workouts in the summer. Manning tried again with a sign reading, "Mandatory VOLUNTARY Workouts."

The coaches banned those as well. Manning was frustrated. He later said he should have tried an alternative tactic with a sign reading, "Keg party, 5:30 p.m. Bring your cleats!" If he had thought of that, Manning half-joked, "there wouldn't have been a single no-show."[16]

Didn't anybody realize that Peyton just wanted to get better and he just wanted his teammates to get better?

NOTES

1. Jimmy Hyams, *Peyton Manning—Primed and Ready* (Lenexa, KS: Addax Publishing Group, 1998), 97.

2. Ibid., 98.

3. Mark Stewart, *Peyton Manning—Rising Son* (Brookfield, CT: Millbrook Press, 2000), 22.

4. Archie Manning, Peyton Manning, and John Underwood, *Manning* (New York: HarperEntertainment, 2000), 265.

5. Hyams, *Peyton Manning,* 98.

6. Ibid., 103.

7. Tim Polzer, *Peyton Manning: Leader On and Off the Field* (Berkeley Heights, NJ: Enslow Publishers, 2006), 56–57.

8. Hyams, *Peyton Manning,* 99.

9. Tom Mattingly, *Tennessee Football—The Peyton Manning Years* (Charlotte, NC: UMI Publications, 1998), 53.

10. Ibid., 30.

11. Hyams, *Peyton Manning,* 103.

12. Ibid., 105.

13. Ibid., 107.

14. Ibid., 108.

15. Manning, Manning, and Underwood, *Manning,* 258.

16. Ibid., 267.

Archie Manning (center) is flanked by his NFL quarterback sons Peyton (left), of the Indianapolis Colts, and Eli, of the New York Giants, during a Nerf Father's Day promo, June 14, 2008, in New York. Archie Manning used to play a game with his sons called "Amazing Catches," where he'd throw the ball just out of their reach and they'd have to make a diving grab. Peyton and Eli have had a lot of amazing passes lately in winning two Super Bowl MVP awards, Peyton in 2007 and Eli in 2008. AP Photo/Stephen Chernin.

Colts quarterback Peyton Manning (left) throws over San Diego Chargers defensive tackle Luis Castillo during the first quarter of an AFC wild-card playoff football game in San Diego, January 3, 2009. AP Photo/Chris Carlson.

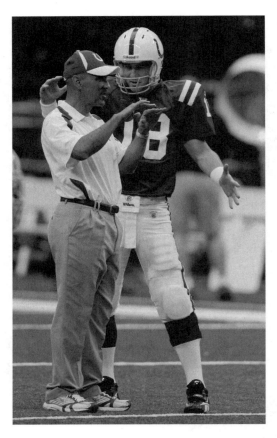

Colts coach Tony Dungy (left) talks with quarterback Peyton Manning during the drills before a preseason NFL football game in Indianapolis, August 28, 2008. AP Photo/Darron Cummings.

Peyton Manning talks about being named the AP's NFL Most Valuable Player in Indianapolis, January 2, 2009. Manning joins Brett Favre as the only three-time winner of the award. Manning also was the league MVP in 2003, when he shared it with Tennessee quarterback Steve McNair, and in 2004. AP Photo/Michael Conroy.

In this October 27, 2008, photo, quarterback Peyton Manning (18) calls a play against the Tennessee Titans in the first quarter of an NFL game in Nashville, Tenn. The Colts never doubted Manning would revert to his old form that season. Manning's second-half performance turned the Colts into the league's hottest team entering the playoffs. AP Photo/ Bill Waugh, File.

University of Tennessee quarterback Peyton Manning crosses the goal line for a third-quarter touchdown during Tennessee's 17-10 win over Vanderbilt on November 29, 1997, in Knoxville, Tennessee. AP Photo/Mark Humphrey.

Peyton Manning drops back in the pocket to make a pass at Pro Player Stadium in Miami, November 8, 1998, in his rookie season. Manning was held to 140 passing yards completing 22 of 42 attempts with two interceptions and one touchdown in the Colts' 27-14 loss. AP Photo/Tony Gutierrez.

Chapter 7

THE BEST IN THE COUNTRY

By his junior year at Tennessee, Peyton Manning had long eclipsed any competition for the quarterback role in the UT backfield. His deeds compared him—favorably—with the acknowledged best collegiate quarterbacks in the nation.

In large measure because of Manning's ability and leadership, Tennessee was being touted as a potential national championship team when the 1996 season began.

Manning did not mind receiving attention for his accomplishments, but he was such a linear, straight-ahead personality that he hated receiving attention for himself or his team based on maybes. Being named to a preseason All-American team was all fluff to him and being a preseason number 1–rated team was equally meaningless. Manning believed in rewards based on performance on the field. The last thing he wanted was to be distracted by accolades based on puffery. When college football experts talked up Tennessee as a likely national champion in 1996, Manning worked double time, alongside coach Phillip Fulmer, to downplay the expectations. Like any conservative football personality, Manning was a one-game-at-a-time guy. As someone who had been around the sport his entire life, he recognized more than most the pitfalls of overconfidence, the regularity of upsets, and just how things spelled out on paper could go awry on the field.

This is another way that overzealous fans differ from a down-to-earth player. Fans read over the schedule before the season and chalk up wins and losses on the record before the games are played. A wise player won't get more than one week ahead in his thoughts. Still, plenty of players read their press clippings and believe the build-'em-up advertising. It is one thing if they believe it and keep it in perspective. It can be dangerous if they read it and slack off in preparation because they think the game is a "sure thing."

"Number 1 in the country sounds so good, but it's so much better after the season," Manning said. "Coach Fulmer told us early, don't believe the hype. It's hard not to get caught up in that. We had a lot of players who believed it. You want to have confidence, but you want to be humble.... We believed the number 1 ranking and got caught up in that. It ended up hurting us."[1]

Schools that play in very challenging leagues often schedule a game or two in the beginning of the season against a school that in theory should be easy to handle. Once in a while, shocking upsets occur in early September, but much more often the presumed power overwhelms the less-heralded team. The Volunteers opened Manning's junior season with a 62-3 victory over the University of Nevada at Las Vegas. With standing-room followers allowed in, more than 107,000 fans watched the massacre at Neyland Stadium.

The heady descriptions of how great Tennessee was and the nationwide praise may well have affected the Volunteers during their second game against UCLA. Although UT held on for a 35-30 win, the players were brought down to earth. They were fortunate it didn't take a defeat to get the message across about how nothing was going to be handed to them. Manning was an efficient 16 for 28 for 288 yards and one touchdown.

The clock was advancing and UCLA stayed within a touchdown of Tennessee much of the day. Manning felt UT was the better team and had no business losing to the Bruins. He adopted a refuse-to-lose attitude in the fourth quarter and once overruled a play sent in by the coaches from the sideline with an audible call at the line of scrimmage. This was an occasion when Manning's maturity and game savvy, coupled with his exhaustive film study, paid off. He recognized UCLA's defense and changed the play to give the Volunteers an advantage. Joey Kent, Manning's favorite receiver, wiggled free, caught a pass, and darted 53 yards for a score. The play dazzled the Tennessee followers, but undoubtedly Manning would have received a coach's lecture if the play had failed. "It's one of those plays where if you're a veteran, you can change something like that and get away with it—as long as it works," Manning said.[2]

The key phrase in that sentence is "as long as it works." Manning may have been super-duper prepared for any eventuality, but he was not immune from coaches' criticism. He knew that if he was going to overrule the coaches' wishes, he had better be successful. It's not as if Fulmer ever would have benched Manning for changing the play, but he might have put him on a shorter leash, reduced his play-changing authority.

Week number 3 in Manning's junior year brought a major event, one of those circled games on the schedule. After two years of being toppled by Florida, the Volunteers were staking their number 1 ranking against the Gators. The road to the SEC title and the national championship ran through Florida, but Coach Steve Spurrier and Florida seemed to have a stranglehold on the rivalry. Over the years Tennessee was able to beat up on just about everyone else, but then would be wasted by the Gators. It was aggravating and humiliating. Manning hated the situation and he burned to rectify it. He had sucked on a victory cigar when UT put an end to Alabama domination and now he wanted to once again earn a victory cigar by polishing off Florida.

It didn't happen. The Gators still had Tennessee's number. In a frustrating game, Florida ended the Volunteers' run at the top of the polls with a 35-29 victory. The Gators sealed off the Tennessee running attack and it fell to Manning to try to win the game through the air. Manning attempted 65 passes, far more than he did in any other college game. He completed 37 of them for 492 yards gained and four touchdowns. Statistically, those numbers could have indicated a rout in Tennessee's favor, but Manning also threw four interceptions. All of the interceptions came early, while Florida was building a 35-0 lead. Manning's passing heroics pumped up the Volunteers in the second half, but the Gators had just enough bite to edge the Vols.

"It was a habit, losing to Florida," an irritated Manning said.[3]

Several of the individual stats from the Florida game represented school records, and even in defeat Manning was gaining more notoriety, not only in Knoxville but also around the country. A superstar athlete finds it difficult to hide from the public even in New York, Los Angeles, or Chicago. When someone is the biggest-name player on the most popular team in town in a place the size of Knoxville, which has about 180,000 people, it's impossible to pop into the Krystal hamburger stand or stop anywhere in public without being mobbed. At one point, Manning started wearing disguises when he left the UT campus.[4]

If the Florida game was highlighted in special ink on the schedule, then the next week's foe was going to be starred, circled, and written in all capitals. About two and a half years had passed since Peyton Manning made his decision to attend the University of Tennessee and gave the entire state of Mississippi indigestion. Now, his third year as an undergraduate in Knoxville, Manning had to travel to Oxford to play a game and do his mighty best to defeat Ole Miss. Peyton would have been happy to go through his college career without ever visiting Oxford at the helm of another team's offense. Archie would have been just as eager to see Mississippi dropped from Tennessee's schedule for the duration of his son's college days. However, both schools are members of the Southeastern Conference and the league makes the schedule. Both Mannings worried that old wounds would be opened and that bad feelings would stir again.

The game was scheduled for October 3, 1996, but there was more than one twist. The game was chosen as a *Thursday Night Football* attraction on ESPN, so it was not going to be played on one of those glorious, sunny autumn days remembered so fondly by the Mannings. And although Mississippi remained the home team, a major corporation paid the school $1 million to move the game to a slightly more neutral stadium in Memphis. Memphis was in Tennessee, but it was actually closer to Oxford than to Knoxville. One way that the potential for any incidents was minimized was by having Archie sit in a private skybox. He watched the game with best-selling author John Grisham. Grisham lives in Oxford and in one of his novels he named a character after Archie Manning. The fictional Archie Manning was known for his jurisprudence, not his quarterbacking ability.

Archie, well aware of likely media demands, expected to be sought for interviews in the days leading up to the game so he turned into a ghost. He submitted to a few and then packed a suitcase, walked out the door of his home with Olivia on his arm, and went off to a vacation retreat in Destin, Florida, where no reporters could find him. One reporter contacted Archie about two weeks before the game, however, before he left, and he did talk about traveling to Ole Miss to watch his son try to beat his old school, though he revealed little. "I'd just as soon not deal with it," Archie said. "I just don't plan to get in the middle of it. I know a lot of people want opinions on this or that. I don't plan to do that 100 times."[5]

Archie had borne the brunt of the negative feedback when Peyton chose Tennessee over Mississippi. Emotions were still a little bit raw about the treatment he received. Peyton's emotions were hardly placid, either. For years he dreamed of becoming the quarterback for Ole Miss. He understood his dad's love for the campus and school and links to the football team and he had invested his own emotions for years believing that he would one day throw the ball for the Rebels. It hadn't worked out that way. His allegiance was to another school, but he hadn't forgotten all of those years of hearing how terrific Mississippi was. Now he was on his way to play Mississippi while wearing enemy colors. He felt that his number 16 jersey might as well be a bull's-eye.

Archie told Peyton to just play football and not worry about any extracurricular matters. Peyton practiced extra hard in the week leading up to the game, realizing that if he played poorly he might hear about it forever. He heard and knew the favored songs played by the Mississippi band, but he enjoyed it more when the Tennessee band played "Rocky Top." So many Manning journeys to watch Mississippi football were pleasure trips, but Peyton knew that this was all about taking care of business.

"I knew I was going to have mixed emotions," Peyton said. "I know he [his father] was nervous that day. I know he wanted me to play well. I know he wanted Tennessee to win the ballgame because he was pulling for me. People were asking him who he was going for. Well, it was a no-brainer. He was going to pull for his son. But I know it was a rough week for him."[6]

It was not such a rough day for the Tennessee football team. The Volunteers were one of the best teams in the land, but Ole Miss was in rebuilding mode. The game was close at first, 17-3 at the half, but Tennessee steadily pulled away. Peyton's fears of being a bust on the field did not play out. He had a good day, completing 18 of 22 passes for 242 yards and one touchdown. He did not throw an interception. The Vols trampled Ole Miss, 41-3. The confrontation with Mississippi had not been as painful or difficult as Peyton anticipated, but he was also happy it wasn't a best-two-out-of-three series, either. "I'm glad all that's over with," Peyton said. "My dad can sleep the rest of the year."[7]

Peyton gave the game ball to his father and Archie did talk to a few reporters afterwards. "I'm proud of the way he handled the pressure tonight," Archie said.[8] The pressure was not in surviving a close game, but in dealing with an unnecessarily emotionally inflated game. Peyton simply took care of business.

Each week it seemed that something Peyton was involved in turned to gold for the Volunteers. The SEC was never shy on challenges and a quarterback trying to lift his team to a championship had to be on his toes every game. Nothing illustrated that more vividly than a hard-fought win over Georgia 10 days after the Mississippi game. On one play, Manning stepped on his fullback's foot and, while falling to the ground, completed a pass. But that didn't compare to the showcase play. On a day when Manning completed 31 out of 41 attempts for 372 yards, his arm an automatic extension of terrific play calling and execution, the most flabbergasting moment occurred on a broken play.

The Volunteers had advanced the ball to the Georgia 5-yard line and needed just inches for a first down. The Bulldogs stacked the front line with behemoth tackles that far outgrew real bulldogs in size. The call from the Tennessee sideline was a run—right into the heart of the growling defense. Not even Brent Gibson, Manning's center, about to snap him the ball, thought that Peyton would be able to penetrate the line on a keeper up the middle. Peyton said later that Gibson actually said, "Uh, oh," when he came up to the line of scrimmage. Manning took the hike and put his shoulder down to plunge into the line. His blockers did not push the opposition out of the way. But the Georgia rushers didn't reach him for a tackle either. Manning knew he had not gained the few inches, but he also had not heard the play whistled dead by officials. So it was a live ball and he had second life. Instead of trying to push forward again, Manning retreated. Georgia rushers flooded through the Tennessee line and began chasing him. Manning started running again, although this time it was backwards. Back, back, back he ran, much like ESPN commentator Chris Berman's home-run call. Manning also rolled a bit to his right, to his throwing side.

Horrified coaches and fans watched as Manning retreated to the 23-yard-line, courting a loss of 18 yards. He was still going, albeit more to the right than back, when he paused, looked downfield, spotted receiver Marcus Nash, and heaved a pitch into the end zone. Nash made a flamboyant grab and Tennessee scored a touchdown on a hopelessly broken play that was critical in the 29-17 win.

Proving that not only was his body intact after eluding the potentially crushing rush, but his sense of humor was as well, the first thing Manning said when he reached the Tennessee sidelined and looked at his coaches was, "Great call." Fulmer responded, "What the hell am I supposed to tell the media?" And a rather smug Manning replied, "Tell them it was a called play."[9]

The year before, Manning had made one of Tennessee fans' fondest wishes come true by leading the Volunteers to a rout of Alabama. Alabama II loomed next. Breaking the losing streak was one thing, but establishing a winning streak was quite another for the Vols against the Crimson Tide. Alabama was never going to be a pushover. Alabama would be spoiling for revenge and be additionally motivated as an underdog against highly rated Tennessee. More often the situations were reversed. These were the games Manning imagined playing in, against teams with tradition that were beloved in their home bases throughout the SEC. He thrived on the match-ups against teams like Alabama and there was never a chance he would take those teams' capabilities for granted. This time Tennessee prevailed, 20-13, a closer game to be sure, but the win was posted in the proper column and that was good enough for Manning.

If there was a team that the Volunteers did take for granted in 1996, it was Memphis State. The Tigers were an instate rival because of proximity, but fans routinely counted Vol encounters with Memphis State as victories. The Tigers were not part of the SEC and figured to be a gnat that would be easily smacked and disposed of. Only the unthinkable occurred. For the first time in 16 meetings, Memphis State upset Tennessee. The final score was 21-17 and nobody could blame the Tigers if they lit up the stogies in their locker room. It was a huge confidence builder for a team that had limited positive historical achievements to call upon and it was a bummer that had major ramifications for the type of bowl game a highly thought-of Tennessee team could expect to play in over the Christmas holidays.

The Volunteers finished off Vanderbilt, another Tennessee school with growing aspirations, in the final regular-season game, 14-7. That left UT at 9-2, a good overall showing, but not worthy of being ranked number 1 or being chosen for one of the fanciest holiday bowl games. Tennessee bested Northwestern of the Big Ten in the Citrus Bowl.

By the end of the season, Manning had amassed a passel of school records. This included becoming the first Tennessee quarterback to go over 3,000 yards in a year. The 3,287 yards that Manning gained through the air broke his own record, set his sophomore year. There was no reason to think that Manning's senior year wouldn't be even better. That is, if there was a senior year. There had been a growing trend for college football players who were recognized as among the best in their class as juniors to come out of school a year early and enter the NFL draft. There was no doubt that Manning's goal was to play pro football and there was no doubt that he would be a top selection if he chose to forego his senior year.

This was no lightly made decision for any underclassman. Some players were in school merely as a training ground to prepare for pro football. That was a given. Those players might not be close to earning a degree. Some players came from homes that faced challenging financial hurdles and by turning pro early they could upgrade the lifestyles of their families. Naturally, there was also the issue of whether or not the junior was physically and mentally prepared to play pro ball, to make the move in the sport from game to profession. Beyond that there was whether or not the pros wanted the player. The player might have the desire to come out of school a year early, but if he wasn't going to be drafted high enough or at all, the move would be a mistake and he would lose out on playing a final year of college ball.

For certain no-doubt future professionals like Manning, there was an impatience to get going, to move to the next level and show what they could do against the best players in the world. There was also the fear that they could suffer a serious injury that would ruin their pro careers before they got started. Some top-tier college players who chose to return for their final season were able to take out pricey insurance policies that safeguarded their future against career-ending injury.

Given that Manning had been receiving compliments about his pro readiness from the time he was a junior in high school it was difficult to argue that he was not ready for the NFL. He was more mature and more prepared than 90 percent of all pro draftees and even though young quarterbacks often found it the most challenging to adapt, if anyone could do so at 21 it was presumed Manning would be the guy.

The week after Tennessee's surprising loss to Memphis State during Manning's junior year, when he was already feeling low, the Volunteers faced Arkansas. During one possession, Manning was tackled hard by a Razorback defender and strained the medial collateral ligament in his right knee. The injury was bothersome, but not exceptionally serious. However, the incident did worry him and Manning began thinking about leaving Tennessee a year early. "I'm thinking, 'Maybe it is time to leave for sure,'" he said.[10] Such language was hardly forceful, sounding like a definite maybe, but at the least it did air the issue.

One thing that holds back serious students from pursuing a professional career early is being close to earning a college degree and fearing that if they leave the college environment they will never return to finish it. Manning, however, had already dealt with that issue. He had started college early by accumulating summer school credits and was on track to graduate in less than four years. He could turn pro without attending Tennessee for another year and he could also walk away with a degree in communications.

By the time the Vols wrapped up Manning's junior season the debate was on the streets. It was no longer just Peyton talking to his family and coaches about whether or not to return, it was every Tennessee fan voicing an opinion about whether he should stay or go, whether he would stay or go. At the end of the Citrus Bowl, the

Tennessee fans began their own lobbying campaign as the team walked off the field at the final gun. "One more year! One more year!" the chants rang out.[11] No one wondered what the orange-clad spectators were asking for.

Tennessee fans were very worried they would lose the centerpiece star of their offense. More and more frequently juniors were coming out of college early to join the NFL and take advantage of the multimillion-dollar contracts being dangled in front of them. Volunteer supporters did not have to have long memories to remember the last time the team faced a similar situation. Only the year prior to Manning's arrival on campus junior quarterback Heath Shuler had opted for the NFL.

The football season ended over Christmas break and Manning returned to school in January. Submerged in his courses as he worked toward finalizing his degree, not a day went by when he did not think about whether he would be back at Tennessee for the 1997 season or if he would be making his debut in the NFL. Although the manner in which Manning would graduate to the pros from college play was drastically different than the path followed from high school to college, in a sense it was like being recruited again. The one key difference was that Manning would have no say in which NFL team drafted him. Whatever team took him would probably be the team with the first overall pick and that meant the worst team in the league. If in the final days of his college selection, Manning reduced the choices to Tennessee versus Mississippi, the contest was a little bit more abstract this time. It was Tennessee versus the NFL. He was making the choice based on a concept. It was staying where he was weighed against a new lifestyle in pro ball, in an unknown city, playing for a team coached by someone he likely didn't know and might not even like.

Was he ready? Manning thought so. He knew he could play. Was he prepared? Again he thought he knew much more than the average rookie. Did he want to leave a place he loved and enjoyed for the unknown? That he wasn't so sure about. He vacillated. One minute he thought he was going pro for sure. The next minute he was going to stay at Tennessee and ride it out. He talked to coaches. He talked to teammates. He talked to friends. He talked to family. He talked to Ashley. Months passed and he had not made a decision. Tennessee needed to know for recruiting purposes whether or not it would have Manning under center for one more year. The NFL had a deadline for declaring whether he would throw his name into the April draft.

Although Manning had started leaning toward the pros after the minor injury suffered in the Arkansas game, he had not crossed the

Rubicon and done anything irrevocable. "I felt unfulfilled [that he hadn't accomplished everything he wanted to playing in college] enough to be having second thoughts about leaving early," he said. "I was bouncing back and forth like a volleyball. I'd be hanging out with players in Knoxville and thinking, 'This is just good. I'm staying.' Then I'd go home to New Orleans and tap into some of the people dad wanted me to discuss it with, and I'd say to myself, 'That's it. I'm going.' Back and forth. Back and forth."[12]

Archie Manning, who had played out four seasons with Mississippi, albeit with the NCAA's freshman-mandated junior varsity in a time period when the NCAA did not allow freshmen to play varsity, did his best to help his son make up his mind. As was his usual method, he backed off and let Peyton think things through on his own. But when Peyton could not decide, his father offered to put him in touch with other football figures who had dealt with similar situations. In choosing a college, Peyton picked the brains of head coaches and their offensive coordinators. During his internal debate about whether or not to play one more year in college he discussed his circumstances with such superstar athletes as Fran Tarkenton, Roger Staubach, Michael Jordan, Troy Aikman, Bernie Kosar, Drew Bledsoe, Rick Mirer, Phil Simms, and a coach, Hank Stram. Most of the sports figures discussed one of the pros or cons for making the choice that Manning had already examined. They just added more perspective. If you stay, you know you could get hurt, Manning was told. If you stay, you might win the Heisman Trophy as the best player in college ball. If you come out early, you will make so much money you won't miss college ball at all. Manning admitted his head was spinning, but the more he talked over his choice, the more he leaned toward going back to Tennessee for his last season.

While it was impossible to determine for certain which NFL team would select Manning in the draft (and he could always be immediately traded to another team as part of a more complicated deal), the New York Jets were holding the number 1 pick. The renowned Bill Parcells was the Jets' head coach and he had expressed admiration for Manning. The appeal of playing in New York and for Parcells tilted Manning a bit in favor of going for it with the NFL.

Ultimately, as the calendar slipped into March, Peyton mentally committed to staying at Tennessee for one more school year. When he told his father the decision was final, Archie made him keep the choice to himself for a few more days until he was absolutely, positively sure. Less than half a day before he was scheduled to make his decision

known to the world at a press conference did Manning give his immediate family the word he was staying in college. Then he telephoned
Vols' coach Phil Fulmer. The late-night call woke Fulmer up, but he
was delighted to hear why he was hearing his quarterback's voice at
1 a.m. when Manning said, "Coach, I'm staying." Fulmer's reaction was
enthusiastic, if somewhat predictable. "I love you man!" Fulmer said
upon hearing the good news.[13]

At a hastily arranged news conference on the afternoon of March 5
in the Ray Mears Room at the Thompson-Boling Arena on the University of Tennessee campus, Manning found a very curious throng.
Reporters were present from many big cities. The news was of such interest to UT football fans that among the estimated 150 media people
was a crew from a local radio station broadcasting the announcement
live. Manning could have ended the suspense by walking in wearing
his orange number 16 football jersey, but instead he gave no hint of
what he was going to do as he entered the room and sat down behind a
microphone. Neither his body language nor his face revealed which
way he was leaning. Then he told the assemblage he was sticking
around Knoxville for one more season. "I looked at the money," he
said, "but remaining a college student was strongest in my heart."[14]

Manning said it was difficult when everyone urged him to hurry and
make up his mind, but he felt he had to work the entire matter out in
his head and with his emotions so he would have no regrets. The decision did not come easily, he noted. "I've thoroughly researched the situation and gathered a great deal of information. I've asked dozens of
people what they thought and I have prayed a lot about it also. I knew
I wanted to be 100 percent sure of my decision."[15]

Although he would still get to play football as he began taking
graduate-level courses with the hope of leading the Volunteers to a
national title and he would try to put together a Heisman Trophy–caliber
season, Manning chose to stay in Knoxville for more intangible reasons.
He was measuring his college career at Tennessee against his father's at
Mississippi and it felt incomplete to not have the final year. All of those
formative years absorbing SEC football culture added up to the turning
point in his decision. It was worth it to Manning (whose family was
financially secure as opposed to many other players' families who
weren't) to pass up the chance to bank millions of dollars right away for
another season being a kid. When a sports reporter at the press conference could not fathom why anyone would defer the opportunity to make
millions of dollars by asking what he was getting by staying, Manning
said, "A scholarship, room and board, and the right to call one play a

game. I also get to drive Coach Fulmer's Lexus." Which was news to Fulmer. The coach had given Manning the keys to the offense, not to his car.[16]

Fulmer offered his own dead-pan humor in response. "He's got to win the job in spring practice," the coach said. Brad Lampley, a Tennessee lineman, said Manning's teammates had pretty much concluded his departure for the pros was a done deal and when he heard that Manning was staying, Lampley said, "That surprised me more than the O.J. verdict."[17] The only thing at that point in their lives Manning and the former Southern Cal Heisman Trophy winner who had been tried and acquitted of murder had in common was their mutual appreciation of football.

A Tennessee employee later called Manning's performance at the press conference "one of his finest hours as a Vol." The reaction was instantaneous from the nonmedia observers in the room—raucous cheers.[18]

A little bit later, Manning said after all of the thinking he had devoted to the decision, he knew once he announced his plan to stay he would never look back and second-guess it.[19] There has never been any evidence that he did.

NOTES

1. Jimmy Hyams, *Peyton Manning—Primed and Ready* (Lenexa, KS: Addax Publishing Group, 1998), 110.

2. Ibid., 111.

3. Archie Manning, Peyton Manning, and John Underwood, *Manning* (New York: HarperEntertainment, 2000), 267.

4. Joanne Mattern, *Peyton Manning* (Hockessin, DE: Mitchell Lane Publishers, 2007), 16.

5. Hyams, *Peyton Manning*, 112.

6. Ibid., 113.

7. Ibid.

8. Tom Mattingly, *Tennessee Football—The Peyton Manning Years* (Charlotte, NC: UMI Publications, 1998), 66.

9. Hyams, *Peyton Manning*, 114.

10. Ibid., 117.

11. Tim Polzer, *Peyton Manning: Leader On and Off the Field* (Berkeley Heights, NJ: Enslow Publishers, 2006), 58–59.

12. Manning, Manning, and Underwood, *Manning*, 268.

13. Ibid., 271.

14. Polzer, *Peyton Manning*, 60.
15. Hyams, *Peyton Manning*, 121.
16. Manning, Manning, and Underwood, *Manning*, 272.
17. Hyams, *Peyton Manning*, 121.
18. Mattingly, *Tennessee Football*, 70.
19. Hyams, *Peyton Manning*, 121.

Chapter 8

A HOT COMMODITY
ONCE AGAIN

Most football fans, players, and observers felt certain Peyton Manning would forego his senior year at the University of Tennessee and jump to the National Football League a year early. He was virtually assured of being the number 1 player chosen and being given a multimillion-dollar contract. The general opinion was that he could not better his stock, so why not go now?

The idea that a student would want to stay a student one more year was almost a foreign concept. Though many applauded Manning's choice, some derided him as a "dummy." At a time when making as much money as possible and just adding to one's fame seemed to be prized above all other things in American society, it was difficult for some to understand Manning's value system. In the end, just as when he picked Tennessee over Mississippi, he had pleased himself.

Manning's announcement that he was going to play one more year for the Volunteers transformed the 1997 college football season. His presence made Tennessee a preseason national title favorite and made him the front-runner for the Heisman Trophy, the award presented annually since 1935 to the pre-eminent college football player in the land. Manning admitted that that unfulfilled goal helped make up his mind about staying, but only peripherally. He stressed that he was most focused on team goals, on winning, on finally beating Florida, and on just lapping up one more year of campus life and one more year of play in the atmosphere of the Southeastern Conference.

Adhering to the same type of methodology he exhibited when he was choosing a college, Manning took a very deliberate approach in examining all of his options. In a hurry-up world he discovered that few other people had such patience and he was constantly asked which way the wind was blowing.

"The most agonizing thing was being asked so many times what I was going to do," Manning said. "The funny thing was, everybody seemed to know before I made my decision. Everybody had their own ideas and I kept telling everybody, 'I might stay. Just give me a chance. Give me a little time.' Nobody thought I might stay. Nobody listened to me when I said I didn't know what I was going to do."[1]

Once the choice was made, as he had promised, Manning never looked back. Consistent with his character, he threw himself completely into preparation for his final college season and Tennessee's potential run at a national championship.

Although Manning had earned his undergraduate degree, under NCAA rules he had to remain in school, so he began working on a master's degree. The average football fan likely thought this was pro forma, but Manning, again consistent with his character and his study habits, took his classes very seriously, though there was never any indication that he was going to shift career plans despite the urging of at least one faculty member. "I told him, 'You really ought to consider getting a Ph.D. and being a professor,'" UT professor Andy Kozar said.[2] Perhaps if Tennessee offered a Ph.D. field of study in quarterbacking Manning might have taken him up on it. Then again, many felt that Manning was already earning such a degree, though without official portfolio.

Manning was very popular in Knoxville. First and foremost he was admired for his football skills. For those who looked beyond his statistics, there was admiration for the way Manning spoke respectfully of teammates and opponents in his press conferences. And for those who were cynical and felt all athletes were in college merely to play their sport and look ahead to pro careers, he offered his response by earning a degree in three and a half years. When he made his against-the-grain decision to stay in school one more year, Manning elevated his stature to previously unrivaled heights. During the 1980s and 1990s, when Michael Jordan was the best basketball player on the planet, a phrase evolved that captured fans' thoughts: "Be like Mike." In Manning's case, after he chose to stay an amateur one more year, Knoxville hospitals said that there was a spike in the number of newborns being named "Peyton" or "Manning" by their parents. They apparently wanted their sons to grow up to be like Peyton.[3]

All of these traits combined to produce an image of Manning as somewhat of a goody two-shoes and a pronouncement from UT coach Phillip Fulmer did nothing to diminish that viewpoint. "You can talk about Peyton for hours and it sounds like some fairy tale."[4]

Manning, of course, was flesh and blood, even if his performances on the gridiron helped anoint him as a god of the game. It was no surprise that the Manning of his senior season was an even more deluxe-model quarterback than Manning of his junior year. He had added more polish and poise and his skills were still improving. One of the major arguments advanced for high-caliber collegiate athletes to turn pro before they finish their eligibility at their schools revolves around finances. Many college athletes with great talent represent the only financial hope their families have of escaping poverty. There may be considerable pressure on those athletes to take the money as soon as it is available and no one in the sports world—least of all Peyton Manning— begrudges them that. But Manning's family did not fit into that category. The Mannings were well off and Peyton's earnings were not expected to be part of the family income. When such athletes are offered the chance to turn pro early the other argument is the threat of injury. What happens to a great athlete who suffers a career-ending injury his senior year and loses out on millions of dollars in potential paydays, as well as the thrill of becoming a professional in his sport? In Manning's case his family took out increasingly valuable insurance policies on his health that would at the least provide him with a tremendous payout if he could not play due to injury.

For each of Manning's last three years in college, his mother and father paid the premiums on pricey insurance policies guarding against his future earnings potential. There was a $1-million insurance policy on Manning as a sophomore, a $5-million insurance policy on him as a junior, and a $7-million insurance policy as a senior. In each instance, a professional Manning would have almost surely earned more money in those years as a pro. "I'm not saying I didn't look at the money," he said. "I'm human. Believe me, I looked at the money."[5]

After the hullabaloo about Manning's decision died down he concentrated on football. He also conceded, "I know for a fact that I can become a better player. I can get bigger, faster and stronger."[6]

Peyton Manning had been put on a pedestal by Tennessee fans, but also by others watching from a distance. He sometimes protested that he was just a regular guy, not Mr. Perfect. Just before his senior year began, however, evidence of Manning's involvement in an awkward incident somewhat tarnished that image of perfection. A former associate trainer took a leave of absence and sued UT for $3 million after she issued a complaint with 300 charges of sexual harassment. The most publicized incident beyond Tennessee's borders, at least, revolved around Manning, who was accused of "mooning" the woman in the trainer's room, pulling down his pants and flashing his backside at her. For most it was unfathomable that the very buttoned-down Manning would engage in such a sophomoric act. Manning admitted to the fact of the act, but said it was a misunderstanding, that it was a prank aimed at another male athlete in the training room.

Manning said he thought he was doing the mooning behind the trainer's back, but she saw him. Later he telephoned, trying to apologize, but the woman's husband would not put her on the phone. Then he sent a letter of apology. "I was clowning around in the training room with a good friend of mine and she happened to see it," Manning said. "By no means was anything directed at her. It was nothing more than a joke toward someone else. My practical jokes have come to an end."[7]

The trainer and the university reached a $300,000 settlement after the charges were reduced to 33, but most of the details in the case and in the Manning incident were never fully explained. Manning was punished by Fulmer, ordered to perform early-morning runs and having his training table privileges temporarily revoked.

Distractions like that were not welcome in Manning's life, or with the season's preparations overseen by Fulmer. Once the Volunteers began playing football for real in the 1997 season, with the clock ticking and the scores counting on the record, Tennessee was revealed as a powerhouse. In the season opener, the Volunteers knocked off Texas Tech, 52-17, and Manning threw for 310 yards and five touchdowns. That was a notable way to start a Heisman Trophy campaign. The next week Manning threw for 341 yards in a 30-24 win over UCLA.

The third game on the schedule presented the challenge Manning had been waiting for, seemingly for years. In his freshman, sophomore, and junior years, Tennessee's biggest frustration had been annual losses to the Florida Gators. Once again Tennessee was highly regarded nationally. Once again the Gators were highly regarded nationally. A last chance to beat Florida was one reason Manning chose to play his senior year.

Most coaches urge their players to keep quiet in the days leading up to the big game. They try to avoid the so-called bulletin-board material—inflammatory newspaper quotes that might be tacked up on the opposing team's locker-room bulletin board. Not so in Gainesville, where words of boasting and confidence floated from players and coach Steve Spurrier. Peyton Manning, they said, was overrated and the Gators knew how to beat him. The words stung and Manning wanted to best Florida more than ever.

The Vols did not get the win they wanted. Florida jumped out to a 14-0 lead and Tennessee could never catch up. The Gators won, 33-20, despite Manning's 353 yards. He threw three touchdown passes, but also two interceptions. A disappointed Manning completed his college career winless against Florida, a circumstance he addressed sarcastically, if somewhat resignedly, in one book, describing the final try this way: "The next week we went back to Gainesville for our annual loss to Florida."[8]

The Florida defeat could have sent the Volunteers into a negative spiral. Not only did the loss damage Tennessee's prospects of winning a national title in only the third game of the season, but the Gators' triumph gave them the advantage in the race to capture the SEC title. A dispirited Tennessee club could have easily packed it in, thinking that both of the primary team goals had been stolen from them in a single 60-minute appearance. But Tennessee and Manning rallied instead. This was a pivotal moment and called for leadership. Manning was as bummed out as the next player about the loss—maybe more so since the game had taken on personal implications.

It wasn't difficult for Manning to get up for the next week's opponent. Mississippi followed Florida, so he wasn't going to have a letdown. An easy 31-17 win over the Rebels (Manning threw for 324 yards) righted the Volunteers' ship and they set out to prove that the preseason suggestions of them being worthy of a top-five ranking were not exaggerated. Georgia, Alabama, South Carolina, Southern Mississippi, and Arkansas all fell like dominoes. While celebrating on the field after the Alabama win, the Tennessee band leader spied Manning and passed him the conductor's baton. So Manning took over new play-calling duties. It didn't take long before he realized he was better at directing the offense than the band, however, and he gave up, waving to the crowd instead of the horn section.

"I'm never going to have a chance to do it again," Manning said. "I didn't hesitate at all. How many people can say they directed the UT band?"[9] Manning pointed out that this was one of those college moments he would have missed out on if he had turned pro a year early.

After the Volunteers were rolling again, Kentucky appeared on the schedule. Of all the outstanding performances in Manning's college career, the game against the Wildcats was probably his finest. Manning passed for 523 yards. He threw for five touchdowns while throwing zero interceptions in the 59-31 victory. Afterwards, Archie Manning teased Peyton with the comment, "You couldn't get 17 more yards?"[10] Archie owned the SEC record for total offense in a game with 540 yards.

Tennessee finished off Vanderbilt for its eighth straight win following the Florida game. And with a second-in-a-lifetime chance, Manning directed the school band, rocking to the sounds of "Rocky Top." He was turning into a regular "Music Man." Circumstances changed over the rest of the regular season. Florida was out of the championship picture and when Tennessee qualified for the SEC championship game in Atlanta, the opponent was a rugged Auburn team, one of the SEC squads the Volunteers did not face during the regular season. The Tigers and Volunteers engaged in a tough battle, but Tennessee won, 30-29. Manning completed 25 out of 43 passing attempts for 373 yards and four touchdowns.

The Tennessee win gave the school its first SEC championship since 1990 and Manning the first championship of his football career. With an 11-1 record, the number 3–ranked Volunteers were chosen to play number 2–ranked Nebraska in the Orange Bowl on New Year's Day, a bigger prize by any measure than the Citrus Bowl. The Tennessee players had the run of downtown Atlanta that night and wherever they congregated they broke into reprises of "Rocky Top." Manning said many UT fans who recognized him thanked him for playing another year. He responded, "Listen, I'm the one who's thankful. I wish I could stay another four years." That wasn't going to happen unless he changed his mind and became a professor after all.[11]

The NFL had been ready for Peyton Manning a year earlier. After additional viewings, anyone who relished fine quarterbacking play wished for a chance to draft him. Manning was regarded as a finished product as ready as anyone would ever be to step right in as a pro starter as a rookie. "I think he's phenomenal," said Denver Broncos' assistant coach Gary Kubiak, a quarterbacking expert. "He makes every throw. His mechanics are second to none."[12]

Manning's senior year passing statistics were eye-catching. He completed 287 passes for 3,819 yards. It should be recalled that he had set the UT record for yards gained passing in a single season with roughly 1,000 fewer when he was a sophomore. Manning's 11,201 yards passing in his career set a new SEC record.

Manning, as Kubiak put it, had completed a phenomenal season, yet in the closing weeks of the regular season, there had been more and more media talk that Michigan's all-purpose defensive back and kick returner Charles Woodson was more deserving of the Heisman Trophy. There appeared to be a sudden groundswell of support for the comparatively unheralded Wolverine star. Michigan had zoomed to the number 1 ranking and was poised to claim the national title. The victor in the Tennessee-Nebraska game could surpass Michigan if the Wolverines lost, but that was not expected to occur.

Meanwhile, in the weeks between the SEC title game and the Orange Bowl, Manning, who had been so durable during his college career, faced a new problem. The morning after the win over Auburn and the celebration with his teammates, Manning awoke in his hotel room with a swollen right knee. It was not insignificant swelling; the hinge had ballooned out in somewhat unreal fashion. Manning initially could not recall how he even hurt the knee, but then thought back to one play during the Auburn encounter. Manning had smacked his knee hard on the artificial turf while he was lunging to make a tackle on an Auburn runner who was returning a Tennessee fumble. Although hurting a bit he had finished the game and thought of the ache in the knee as nothing more than a routine bruise.

"I could barely get out of bed," said Manning, noting the knee looked like "a watermelon." The damage was far more than a bruise, but Manning didn't realize that at first.[13] The diagnosis was a burst bursa sac. The harsh, flush impact of the knee slamming the turf did cause the injury.

During the few-week gap between the end of the college football regular season and the wrap-up with Christmas and New Year's bowl games, the sport bestows its most prized awards to the best overall players, the best defensive backs, best linemen, and the like. The most coveted award is the Heisman Trophy, presented by the Downtown Athletic Club in New York, to the player considered the finest all-around player in the land for that season. Five finalists are assembled for the announcement, but realistically no one felt there were more than two genuine contenders. Manning had been the favorite from the moment he announced he would return for his senior year. Woodson was a latecomer in the thought process who seemed to gain momentum in the final month of regular-season play.

Manning left for New York a day after the SEC title game, foregoing treatment and rest for his knee. The Heisman presentation was the most suspenseful off-field moment of the 1997 college football season. To the surprise of many and the dismay of Tennessee fans, the trophy went to Woodson. Voters, from sportswriters to past winners, chose Woodson over Manning in a process that had been monitored throughout the season. Manning said he knew he was losing his own momentum to be considered the best when he had his greatest day in college against Kentucky with those 523 yards gained and yet dropped in the poll.

"I'd be lying if I said I wasn't disappointed finishing second to Charles Woodson," Manning said, "but at that point I didn't expect it, and when Woodson's name was called it was no surprise. I'd already gotten a strong feeling for how it worked, mostly as confirmation of doubts I'd heard expressed by others."[14]

Although the Heisman is the best-known and most esteemed award given out for the "best" player, the Maxwell Award is also presented with essentially the same criteria and Manning was the recipient of that. Manning was also awarded the Draddy Award as the NCAA Division I Scholar Athlete (accompanied by a $135,000 payment to UT), an $18,000 postgraduate scholarship, the Davey O'Brien Award as the nation's top quarterback, and the Johnny Unitas Golden Arm Award. Manning was named to every All-American team chosen and Tennessee retired his number 16 jersey. Manning also appeared on the *David Letterman Show*. After Manning's quips left the host laughing, Letterman said, "The kid has writers." Back in Knoxville, a street on campus was named "Peyton Manning Pass" after the departing quarterback. It was no mountain pass, but a 100-yard pathway the football team walks over leading to Neyland Stadium from the athletic complex. A life-sized Manning mannequin was created as part of a Tennessee Hall of Fame exhibit. A baby giraffe born at the Knoxville Zoological Gardens was named Manning. It was not named after Archie, and Peyton does have a slightly elongated neck.[15]

Manning was circumspect in public and gracious to Woodson at the Heisman Award ceremony, but admitted disappointment in not winning the top honor. "I'd be less than honest if I said I didn't want to win the Heisman for the people back home in Tennessee," he said. "In a lot of ways, I wanted to win it for them because they've been so supportive throughout my four years. I apologize to them. I wouldn't change a thing about the past year, or anything in my career. I did the best I could all year long and that's all I wanted to do."[16]

Just when Manning thought there was no other award he was eligible for that could be bigger than the Heisman Trophy, he was shocked to be rewarded with the Sullivan Award as the United States' top amateur athlete in any sport. Amateur Athletic Union President Bobby Dodd said of Manning, "Peyton exemplifies the best true amateur athlete in all of sport with a commitment to his education and to sportsmanship."[17]

In addition to his accomplishments on the football field, his strong academic standing, and his earning his degree in less than four years, Manning demonstrated his commitment to the community and the philanthropic nature that also pleased Sullivan selectors. Manning often made speeches in schools around Knoxville stressing the importance of education and the need to stay away from drugs and violence. He also regularly visited hospital patients of all ages and coped with the strong emotions provoked by visiting terminally ill children.

Manning was visibly moved by the presentation of the Sullivan Award and delivered an acceptance speech at a luncheon in Knoxville. "It's really very humbling when a person is selected to receive an award for something he loves to do," Manning said. "It's even more rewarding for me to receive the Sullivan Award today because its voters traditionally look beyond statistics and highlights; instead they look at the person and what he or she represents."[18]

As a student, Manning compiled a 3.61 grade-point average on a scale of 4.0 and earned a degree in speech communication—likely something that would come in handy when conducting all of the interviews he figured to give as a professional football player. He achieved Phi Beta Kappa status and received a University of Tennessee Chancellor's Citation for "Extraordinary Campus Leadership and Service." In addition, Manning took the $18,000 he had been awarded for graduate study and created his own scholarship fund for a worthy Tennessee high school student who wished to attend UT. The Peyton Manning Scholarship is awarded annually.

Nearly as much off-field attention cascaded down on Manning as had when he was running up and down the field for the Volunteers. However, he still had one game remaining, the looming, important Orange Bowl. While Manning gallivanted around the country instead of resting and treating his knee, the injury unexpectedly worsened. Manning's knee became infected and he had to be hospitalized for five days. When Manning should have been fine-tuning his game and the Tennessee offense for its clash against formidable Nebraska, he was flat on his back. Even after he was released from the hospital, Manning's knee remained swollen and he did not practice at all.

In a Tennessee fan's worst nightmare, Manning was listed as questionable for participation in the Orange Bowl and he packed street clothes to wear on the sideline if he couldn't play. He was not cleared to play until two days before the game, which was actually scheduled for January 2, 1998, rather than New Year's Day. Manning was shackled with a knee brace for the game in Miami and was not at peak strength. As Nebraska flexed its muscles and the game slipped away— the Volunteers lost 41-17—Manning seemed less and less able to perform like his usual self. He eventually went to the bench and his backup, Tee Martin, finished the game. Manning's UT career ended with a defeat in an 11-2 season. Number 1 Michigan had defeated Washington State and claimed the national title anyway.

"Nebraska was too strong, too good, too everything," Manning said. "It was a downer for an ending, and in deference to the injury, I passed up all the post bowl all-star games."[19]

Tennessee supporters were still angry about Manning being snubbed for the Heisman. "I don't understand," Coach Fulmer said. A radio station sold 1,600 t-shirts at $5 apiece designated for charity that read, "Keep Your Stupid Trophy." When the radio people ran out of stock a store took over, printing and selling another 1,500. In all $5,000 was raised for a charity called Dream Connection. The organization, much like the Make-A-Wish-Foundation, helps seriously ill children realize their dreams. Honor after honor came Manning's way from UT and Tennesseans.

"Tennesseans made much more of me than I deserved after that final game," Manning said.[20]

The regular season blurred into the SEC championship game, which brought the injury that worsened during the awards season, and took Manning right into the Orange Bowl where his on-field Tennessee career ended. Honors followed him into the winter, culminating with the Sullivan Award luncheon in February, and talk heated up and intensified immensely as the April NFL draft approached. For most it seemed that Manning's selection at number 1 was a no-brainer, but much like Charles Woodson's late-season surge of popularity, there was considerable sentiment growing in favor of another quarterback. Ryan Leaf of Washington State had become a college superstar for the Cougars and pro scouts seemed seduced by his recent body of work. Suddenly, Manning and Leaf seemed to be in a dead heat as the likely number 1 and number 2 draft picks.

Teams in the National Football League are assigned to pick collegians in the annual player draft in inverse order to their success. The team with the worst record gets to choose first. The team that wins the Super Bowl picks last. The Indianapolis Colts had "earned" the right to pick first. Their 3-13 record during the 1997 season demonstrated just how badly they needed an influx of fresh talent. The next-worst team, which inherited the number 2 pick, was the San Diego Chargers. Pro teams often draft for need, meaning if they have a key vacancy in the lineup they are likely to select the best player available at that position rather than necessarily the best player of any size or shape. Both the Colts and the Chargers needed quarterbacks, so for months leading up to the draft it was a foregone conclusion that the top two picks were going to be Peyton Manning and Ryan Leaf. The only issue was which player was going to end up with which team. There is considerable prestige—not to mention top dollar—in being the first player picked in the college draft.

Manning had a deeper résumé and body of work for a team to study. Leaf was coming on like gangbusters. Leaf stood 6-foot-5 and weighed 245 pounds. Manning stood 6-foot-5 and weighed 230 pounds. Both of them had the size teams liked in the pocket and both had powerful arms. Like Manning, Leaf had set passing records, among them throwing for a Pac-10 record 33 touchdowns as a junior and as a senior leading the Cougars to their first Rose Bowl in 67 years. Leaf was nearly as popular in Pullman, Washington, as Manning was in Knoxville, Tennessee, and had finished third in the Heisman voting.

"It's like trying to figure out which is better, vanilla or chocolate," said Colts general manager Bill Polian in a comparison between Manning and Leaf.[21]

There were some suggestions that Leaf's throwing arm might be a tiny bit stronger—rocket to cannon—but when Manning visited teams for private workouts the month before the draft, he dispelled that question. For the most part, the football experts writing about the draft and the administrators of the teams that were going to pick in the draft seemed to be on the same page: whichever quarterback was drafted first, both of the players should have impressive NFL careers. They both seemed likely all-stars down the line once they gained experience and developed.

After four years as starting quarterback at Tennessee, after becoming an All-American, a Heisman finalist, and a sought-after top NFL draft pick, Manning had an extraordinarily high "Q" rating or recognizability factor. He had been on television as an athlete and as a talk-show guest. His every pass had been dissected by sports writers. His face had been shown on the cover of so many magazines that brother Cooper teased that to find any magazine without his sibling, "I finally had to buy Playgirl."[22]

Yet, if anything, the attention was magnified as the April 18, 1998, NFL draft approached. Private workouts are private, but usually word gets out if a top prospect has been invited to show what he's got to a team. Manning did his thing for the Indianapolis Colts and met owner Jim Irsay. Manning was on the cusp of one of the most important moments of his life. For years, he had planned and prepared to be the best quarterback he could be. He had been on the national stage for four years and knew what he could do. Those who knew the pro game had been complimenting him for years. So Manning had no doubts about his ability to lead and play the position. He was convinced he was the best at his position.

After a private session of a different sort, talking with Irsay after the millionaire flew Manning to Florida to get to know him, Manning said, "I think he liked me. I know I liked him. So as I was leaving, I said, 'You know, Mr. Irsay, I'll win for you.'" Irsay later said Manning's words made an impression on him.[23] "They sent shivers down my spine. I knew then he was the guy I wanted," Irsay said.[24]

Meanwhile, Ryan Leaf was making the same type of tour of pro camps, being tested and probed, quizzed and analyzed. He made no enemies on these visits. He performed well and no red flags were raised that he did not belong in such exalted company. He seemed like a worthy first pick if Manning was not the man. There was no reason to drop Leaf to lower than second in anybody's estimation. Manning or Leaf? Leaf or Manning? The debate raged and continued right up until draft day.

Won over by Manning's personality, as well as his statistics, history, and workout performance, the Colts stepped to the podium in New York and announced they were taking Peyton Manning with the first pick in the 1998 NFL draft. San Diego immediately selected Leaf. Both seemed likely to be the quarterback of the future for two downtrodden teams. The teams had just banked their respective futures on their selections. Irsay and Polian cited Manning's intangibles, maturity and poise, as well as talent, as things that set him apart and convinced them to choose the Tennessee grad number 1. "Peyton is a franchise quarterback," Irsay said.[25]

Manning was thrilled to be chosen number 1 overall in the pro draft. It mattered little where a player was drafted if he became a star, but it was a distinction that Manning appreciated. "It's an exciting day," he said. "You're starting one career and saying goodbye to another."[26]

One philosophy applied to breaking young quarterbacks into the NFL wars is to let them sit on the bench and watch the action for a season. That theory grows from the awareness that the pro game is much faster than the college game and it is easy to destroy the confidence of a rookie thrown to the wolves too soon. Comparatively rarely is a freshly drafted quarterback thought to be ready to compete from the opening of training camp. The combination of the great respect they had for Manning's savvy and the lack of any suitable alternative on the roster meant that the Colts were going with the sink-or-swim approach. Manning was going to be thrown in over his head and everyone hoped he could adapt quickly, swim strongly, or at the very least tread water.

Manning would not have been Manning if he had not relished that challenge. He had brought the same approach to college. Tennessee wasn't going to hand him the starting quarterback job as a freshman, but Manning believed given half a chance he could seize it. And he did so.

"We're putting him in there right away," Colts coach Jim Mora said. "We didn't draft this guy number 1 to sit on the bench."[27]

When Archie Manning was coming out of the University of Mississippi in 1971 he was drafted second overall by the New Orleans Saints, but although he was also one of the quarterbacks rushed into the lineup, he felt there was no comparison between his know-how and preparedness for the NFL and his son's. "Peyton is so much farther along than I was when I came into the league," Archie Manning said. "He's ready for this challenge."[28]

As word spread about the large number of Tennessee babies being named "Peyton" after his brother, Cooper, always the one to look for humor in a situation compared it to having a giraffe named for the quarterback. "Peyton's bumped up to human status," Cooper said, "which I guess is a plus."[29]

The man whose true alternative career could have been as a movie critic based on his enthusiasm for watching football film planned to approach his new assignment with the same commitment he had shown when he moved up from high school to college. He was going to watch film until his eyes were bloodshot. Manning wanted to be appropriately compensated as the top pick in the draft, but he absolutely did not want to become a holdout, haggling over his contract status while missing off-season workouts and training camp. He wanted to sign on the dotted line and be done with it, then just focus on football.

From the moment he was drafted, Manning had the chance to become the Colts' best quarterback since Johnny Unitas. Over the years, the Colts had started games under center with Mark Herrmann, Jack Trudeau, Art Schlichter, Gary Hogeboom, Mike Pagel, Browning

Nagle, Craig Erickson, and many others less famous. The Colts were searching for long-term stability and Manning was looking for long-term security.

Manning had always looked ahead and planned ahead. Now he was at the top of the food chain. The opportunity was there to run a pro team, just as he had always imagined. The little boy who had watched his father play in the National Football League was all grown up and about to embark on the same career path as his famous dad. Peyton Manning had waited an extra year rather than be tempted into the NFL early. He had still been the number 1 overall pick and he was going to make millions of dollars.

"My career at Tennessee has been special," Manning said. "I hope to have a better career at Indianapolis."[30]

NOTES

1. Jimmy Hyams, *Peyton Manning—Primed and Ready* (Lenexa, KS: Addax Publishing Group, 1998), 123–24.

2. Mark Stewart, *Peyton Manning—Rising Son* (Brookfield, CT: Millbrook Press, 2000), 23.

3. Ibid., 24.

4. Ibid., 25.

5. Hyams, *Peyton Manning,* 128.

6. Ibid., 129.

7. Ibid., 130.

8. Archie Manning, Peyton Manning, and John Underwood, *Manning* (New York: HarperEntertainment, 2000), 272.

9. Hyams, *Peyton Manning,* 147.

10. Ibid., 149.

11. Manning, Manning, and Underwood, *Manning,* 273.

12. Stewart, *Peyton Manning,* 25.

13. Manning, Manning, and Underwood, *Manning,* 273.

14. Ibid., 275

15. Tom Mattingly, *Tennessee Football—The Peyton Manning Years* (Charlotte, NC: UMI Publications, 1998), 77.

16. Ibid., 79.

17. Ibid., 128.

18. Ibid., 129.

19. Manning, Manning, and Underwood, *Manning,* 274.

20. Ibid., 278.

21. Stewart, *Peyton Manning,* 32.

22. Hyams, *Peyton Manning,* 207.

23. Tim Polzer, *Peyton Manning: Leader On and Off the Field* (Berkeley Heights, NJ: Enslow Publishers, 2006), 65.

24. Hyams, *Peyton Manning,* 220.

25. Polzer, *Peyton Manning,* 65.

26. Stewart, *Peyton Manning,* 36.

27. Ibid., 36.

28. Polzer, *Peyton Manning,* 66.

29. Hyams, *Peyton Manning,* 216.

30. Ibid., 219.

Chapter 9

RIGHT INTO THE FIRE

The Indianapolis Colts were not kidding. They installed Peyton Manning as the starting quarterback for the 1998 season the moment he was officially picked number 1 in the draft. There was a lot of hand-shaking and celebrating in the immediate aftermath and Manning did the obligatory posing for photographs with a Colts baseball cap on his head and a Colts game jersey held up in front of his chest. No one would have been surprised if Colts president and general manager Bill Polian had slipped Manning a playbook during the hubbub and if the quarterback had swiftly retreated to a hotel room to begin studying it.

That did not occur, but given the anxiousness of both parties to get started on the business of learning the pro game and winning football games it could have.

After a dismal showing in 1997 the Colts hired a new coach for 1998. Jim Mora, who had previously coached the New Orleans Saints, knew Archie Manning well, and had watched Peyton grow up, was the new boss. He certainly embraced the idea of starting his new job with Peyton Manning at the controls.

"He's an excellent football player and he's a quality young man," said Mora. "I do know him well. He spent a lot of time around our organization. We know the family well. He's an excellent young prospect."[1]

Soon after being drafted, Manning said he wanted to sign a contract quickly to make sure he did not miss any time practicing with the Colts as he tried to get the feel of being a pro quarterback. Yet Manning was also worth a bundle and he and his family wanted to see him get fair compensation. The details of his first contract with the Colts took a little bit longer to work out than he had anticipated. Eventually, his deal was finalized and, counting incentives, Manning could earn $48 million over six years. When the breakdown was analyzed, sports writers figured out that Manning would be paid roughly $8,000 a play, or around $14,400 per pass attempt. When Archie Manning turned pro in another era (and he was selected number 2 in the draft), his first contract called for $410,000 over five years. Clearly, he was making more than the average American in 1971, but like other things in society, the price of quarterbacks had been hit by inflation.

Peyton Manning was not a big spender by nature, but his first purchase with his newfound wealth was a $200 pair of cowboy boots. He then ponied up for brother Cooper's honeymoon with wife Ellen, acting with mock surprise when the couple went to Paris instead of the "redneck Riviera" along the Florida Panhandle. He also jokingly complained that when he returned to New Orleans to hang out with his friends from high school, "nobody else reaches for the check."[2]

When Manning received a check from the Colts for $2 million he put it all in the bank and forgot about spending—with one major exception. Manning swiftly created a charitable organization called the PeyBack Foundation, which began disbursing funds in 1999 and continues to operate and distribute grants to a wide variety of civic and community groups today. Among the many groups to receive grants from Manning's foundation are the Indiana Youth Institute, the Police Athletic League of Indianapolis, Boys & Girls Clubs of Southeast Louisiana, and the Emerald Youth Foundation of Knoxville, Tennessee. The entire focus is to aid groups that help children. Sometimes the foundation provides Christmas gifts to needy kids. The foundation has also started the PeyBack Bowl high school football event at Indianapolis's RCA Dome, a series of games that raises money for the foundation. By its fifth year it raised $440,000 for the foundation to spend and in its sixth year in 2008 it raised another $380,000.

In its first year of existence, the PeyBack Foundation distributed $900,000 in grants. Since then it has expanded its reach steadily with events that benefit needy families at dinners and in providing food. In 2004 more than 800 people received a holiday meal of turkey, ham, mashed potatoes, and more through the PeyBack Foundation. The foundation also provides 50 tickets per game to disadvantaged children to attend Colts home games, where they receive t-shirts and vouchers for free snacks at concessions stands.

By 2007 the PeyBack Foundation had donated $1.3 million to various charities and service organizations, including $115,000 to Hurricane Katrina relief. On September 6, 2007, St. Vincent's Hospital in Indianapolis renamed its children's hospital the Peyton Manning Children's Hospital at St. Vincent's. Manning and his wife Ashley gave a sizable but undisclosed donation to the hospital and he has maintained a relationship with the hospital and its young patients since entering the NFL.

These contributions and Manning's other commitments helping the less fortunate, almost from the moment he arrived in the National Football League, have led to receipt of numerous awards of recognition, from the NFL's Byron "Whizzer" White Humanitarian Award and the John Wooden Award by Athletes for a Better World to Most Caring Athlete from USA Weekend and the Walter Payton Man of the Year Award from the NFL. The *Sporting News* also acclaimed Manning as winner of its 2006 "Good Guy" award, saying, "Being a Good Guy has nothing to do with athletic performance and everything to do with charitableness. These are the athletes in the sports we cover who open their hearts, as well as their wallets, to serve the needy and the unfortunate."[3]

Manning's first task with the Colts was to learn how to be a good NFL quarterback. He did not want to enter the team's huddle for the first time during a game the way he had with the Volunteers when a more experienced upperclassman told him to chill out and just call the play. He needed to establish his authority immediately.

As the league's overall number 1 draft pick and as a highly visible All-American who had grown up as the son of a former NFL star, Manning was under the glare of a red-hot spotlight from the moment he took his first snap. He had no illusions about being a rookie who could break in under the radar. He was going to be scrutinized, evaluated, and compared to others to the millionth degree. He could no more escape attention than the presidential nominee of a major political party. Every word Manning uttered and every pass Manning threw were going to be studied by football pundits. In addition, every move he made was going to be compared to Ryan Leaf's performance with San Diego.

Manning had supreme confidence in himself to adapt and grow in the role as starting quarterback for a pro team. His lifelong preparation to assume the position helped considerably. He was ready to use his knowledge and he was not going to be shy about calling audibles at the line of scrimmage either. If he saw a defensive shift, he would just change the play on the spur of the moment. Heck, he had been doing that since he teamed with Cooper at Isidore Newman. What gained Manning extra attention as he made his changes in the play was the demonstrative style he brought to the task. It also produced a few chuckles. Manning showed off more hand jive than a 1960s Motown singing group. He flashed more signals than a Navy semaphore. He pointed here and there and everywhere. Of course, when defenders stopped laughing, they also had no idea where the play was going.

Manning felt that he had benefited from his fourth year at Tennessee, that playing one more year at a high collegiate level gave him useful extra experience. "Experience is the best teacher," he said. "Someone told me I'd struggle in my rookie year anyway. I figure I'll struggle less. I did everything I could possibly do to prepare myself in college."[4]

Manning was 22 years and five months old when the Colts began their season on September 6, 1998, only a month older than his father was when he made his rookie debut in 1971. The appearance made Peyton Manning the seventh-youngest player to start at quarterback in NFL history.[5]

When Colts officials committed to Manning, it wasn't clear that they were never going to take him out at all, but that's pretty much how the season went. In all, Manning threw 575 passes in Indianapolis's 16-game season. The only other Colt pass thrown in 1998 was on an option play by a wide receiver. The Colts might as well not have had backup quarterback Bill Musgrave in uniform that season for as much action as he saw. Musgrave, a veteran who was talked out of retirement primarily to be an advisor to Manning that year, was by design more of a tutor than a player.

As had been suspected—and gambled on—Manning proved to be a mature rookie who played older than his age. In a season that would be the envy of most veterans, Manning completed 326 passes. He threw for 3,739 yards and 26 touchdowns. The one sign of overanxiousness and youth that showed up as a failing was Manning's periodic inclination to throw the ball into coverage. As a result he threw 28 interceptions. It was the one statistic that showed he still needed work in acclimating to one of the most demanding jobs in sports. Manning's numbers represented numerous Colts and league rookie records. The old record of 24 touchdown passes by a rookie was set by former New York Giant Charlie Conerly 50 years earlier.

Manning threw for three touchdowns in a game four different times as a rookie and his high yardage for a game was 357 against the

Baltimore Ravens. Four times he threw for more than 300 yards in a game. Miracles are produced in limited quantities in the National Football League, however, and despite the addition of Manning, the Colts demonstrated no improvement in their won-loss record. They once again finished 3-13. New coach, new quarterback, same old Indianapolis record. The fans were going to have to be patient. So was the quarterback, who was not happy about the team's finish or his excessive number of interceptions. Seemingly oblivious to the impact he made on the record book as a rookie, Manning could not stop thinking about the team defeats.

"Bummer," he said near the end of the season. "All we can do is go back to work and try to get better. I really didn't know where I would be at this point. My main goal all season has been to improve each week and realize that this thing could be like a roller coaster."[6]

Seattle Seahawks coach Dennis Erickson had seen Manning in a preseason exhibition and then studied film of him later in the year when his team was about to face the Colts. He couldn't get over the difference over a span of a few months about how Manning had changed. "It's like night and day," Erickson said. "It's unbelievable. You watch how he's grown. You knew that was going to happen eventually, because he's a good athlete."[7]

In all of the debates about the respective abilities of Manning and Leaf only rarely was heard an additional argument in favor of the Colts choosing Manning with the top draft pick. This was from the viewpoint that pro football was, after all, a business. A Louisiana-based draft analyst named Mike Detillier thought with all other things being more or less equal, the Colts should grab Manning. "Peyton Manning will put more people in the seats than Ryan Leaf," Detillier said. "He's the most recognizable athlete to come out of college football since Herschel Walker. The Colts don't have a marquee player on the team."[8]

No Indianapolis team official ever gave that reason for picking Manning over Leaf, but Detillier was prescient. The moment the Colts chose Manning their season-ticket base grew and Manning merchandise, notably his new number 18 jersey, began selling in Indiana as if it were a Beanie Baby.

Week after week, month after month, after the bowl season wrapped up in January of 1998, Manning and Leaf were like Siamese twin quarterbacks joined at the throwing arm when it came time for team officials, scouts, and sports writers to dissect the April NFL draft. Manning or Leaf? Leaf or Manning? Manning had been on the radar screen early and was hyped early for the Heisman before losing out to Charles

Woodson. The situation was analogous with Leaf and the draft. Manning had been in the public eye and was a hotter prospect for a longer time. This time the vote went the other way, Manning was chosen ahead of Leaf.

The Colts' selection of Manning with the first pick turned out to be a real stroke of genius and good fortune. Although Manning and Leaf were judged to be of nearly identical value by expert after expert, the comparison ended right after the draft. Manning was an instant star. Leaf was an instant bust. And he never got better. Perhaps never has there been a starker result between two top choices heralded as being equal in the history of the National Football League draft. An incident the previous February described by Colts coach Jim Mora took on more meaning in hindsight. Mora mentioned that the Colts had had a two-hour meeting with Manning and planned a similar session with Leaf. "We were supposed to meet with Ryan Leaf last night," he said. "He didn't show."[9] That might have been a warning sign to any future Leaf employer.

At the end of the 1997 season, Leaf was thought to have great NFL potential. Mike Price, the Washington State coach who mentored Leaf, raved about his quarterback's capabilities. "No question about it," Price said. "He's the best. Strong arm. Greater vision. Super confidence. He understands the game we're playing. He's the best. Statistically, athletically, he's the best."[10]

But from the moment he left Washington State Leaf transformed into a player who would be unrecognizable to the coach who praised him. He essentially peaked on draft day as the number 2 choice. After being signed for millions of dollars by the Chargers he provided almost no value in return. It was a stunning development. The scouts were as wrong as could be. In no way did Leaf measure up to Manning once they turned pro.

The Colts had said that one reason they leaned toward Manning was his maturity, but no one expected Leaf to display public bouts of immaturity. Leaf first got into trouble for skipping an NFL orientation symposium for rookies. Leaf had some testy relationships with teammates and was caught on camera screaming obscenities at a print reporter. Still, he was the Chargers' starter, being benched only after nine games when his statistics included two touchdown passes and 13 interceptions. During his second season, Leaf argued vociferously with general manager Bobby Beathard and an assistant coach and was caught lying about a hand injury when he played golf instead of practicing. The Chargers suspended Leaf for four games at one point and he issued a written confession statement reading, "I have been selfish and have let my personal shortcomings get in the way of my professional behavior."[11]

Ultimately, after more distracting off-field behavior and almost no success on it, the Chargers dumped Leaf. He bounced to three other teams and his entire pro experience lasted from 1998 to 2002. At least one source summarized his career with the comment, "He is widely regarded as one of the biggest flops in NFL and professional sports history." MSNBC commentator Michael Ventre called Leaf "the biggest bust in the history of professional sports."[12]

Leaf's lifetime stats compare unfavorably to Manning's single-season rookie stats. Leaf completed 315 out of 655 pass attempts for 14 touchdowns and 36 interceptions while gaining 3,666 yards. Eventually, Leaf became head golf coach and assistant football coach at West Texas A&M and looked back with peace at his brush with pro fame, saying, "When playing football became a job, it lost its luster for me. I kind of got out of the spotlight and life's never been this good."[13]

Leaf's meltdown amazed pro football experts as much as Manning's smooth adjustment did. For Manning, as week after week went by during his rookie season in the NFL, life had never been so good. He was doing what he loved, learning on the job, and although the price of victory proved dear, he was absorbing what it would take to become a long-term success in the toughest football league in the world. Although Manning would never be satisfied with anything less than perfection, others were pleased with his progress.

"The improvement is phenomenal," said Polian of Manning. Polian couldn't have been happier that his draft pick was proving his acumen. "I've never seen improvement like this from a rookie in all my years."[14]

Bill Musgrave had been a journeyman quarterback in retirement when the Colts asked him to let Manning pick his brain for a season. For part of the year he and Manning even shared an apartment. They talked quarterbacking, football, the NFL, and the Colts day and night. Even if in the back of his mind the cocky side of Manning wanted to believe that he had seen it all through film study and on football fields, deep down he knew he still had more to learn. The NFL was a higher league, the game was played faster, and the coaches were paid large sums of money to thwart hot-shot quarterbacks coming out of college who thought they could live on their All-America laurels.

"Defensive coordinators are so innovative," Musgrave said. "Different schemes are popping up almost every week. A quarterback has to deal with all of those things flying around you, and at you."[15]

Manning had grown up dreaming of playing SEC football and then making his mark on the NFL. He did not have a city in mind that ranked as highly as Oxford, Mississippi, or Knoxville, Tennessee, for his pro career. All of the cities in the NFL are larger, more metropolitan and cosmopolitan than those college-dominated communities. Manning knew it could never be the same, but he hoped to approximate his experience.

"I want to go to a team that wants me to be in that city," he said prior to the draft, "where the people want me there also. That's very important to me. Whatever town I go to I'd like to have the same experience I had at Tennessee. Whether that's possible, I'm not really sure."[16]

Compared to a New York, Los Angeles, or Chicago, a Boston or Philadelphia, Indianapolis was a big-small town. It also had no Major League Baseball team and no National Hockey League team. With success, there was a greater chance for Manning to shine and be the dominant athlete in town while not having to dodge paparazzi on the streets or in restaurants.

Still, it wasn't as if Manning was ever going to be anonymous in Indianapolis. During his earliest days with the team Manning was recognized routinely wherever he went, and whenever that occurred fans sought an autograph. One day he was at the airport preparing to go to New Orleans for a visit. In the 30 minutes his plane was delayed he signed 30 autographs and didn't get a chance to read a page of the football book he was carrying. Another time, in a doctor's office, Manning was asked to sign a fan's X-rays. More surprisingly, at church, a fan came prepared with a Manning jersey and a pen and asked for an autograph during the benediction. Manning signed all the requests. He had long ago decided that his father's policy of trying to please everyone on that front was the way to go. "I learned from my dad," Peyton Manning said. "It takes five seconds to smile and be nice. It takes the same amount of time to be a jerk. So smile and be nice."[17]

Indianapolis did fall in love with Manning right away. His performance merited the fan support and his achievements earned acclaim far beyond Hoosierland. Manning was chosen as the rookie quarterback of the year by numerous publications and the NFL after his first season. The pundits of the press box and the officials of the game appreciated Manning's leadership and passing as much as his hometown rooters did.

An additional thing that distinguished Manning's debut season in the pros was the fact that he stood behind center for every single one of the Colts' offensive plays in 1998. It is no small thing to stay healthy in the NFL, especially as a quarterback who is the object of the defense's ire and attack. Sprained ankles, wounded knees, broken fingers, and minor concussions are all routine hazards of the job aside from the more severe injuries that can easily knock a player out for the season. In his first Indianapolis season Manning displayed a durability that became his trademark.

Being dinged up is par for the course in the NFL. It is said that by midseason almost every player is playing hurt. But the hallmark of NFL players is that they continue to play when they are hurt. Being "injured" is defined differently than being "hurt." If a player is injured he is out. If a player is hurt, he slaps on an ace bandage and some adhesive tape or takes a cortisone shot to ease the pain. Playing hurt is the sign of a warrior and is taken as a sign that a player puts the team first. Playing hurt gains respect from teammates.

Any number of times during that first season Manning could have begged off with a minor "owie," or his coaches might have considered resting him. He also made his share of rookie mistakes despite his gaudy statistics, notably throwing too many interceptions, including three in a game. When the season ended Manning thanked Mora for keeping him in the lineup the whole season. "Coach," he said, "I really appreciate your hanging with me this year." Mora replied, "You can't learn from the sidelines, Peyton."[18]

Manning never sought to sit out a single play and he made many big plays on offense. But characteristically, and totally consistent with his past habits, Manning worked hard off the field, and veterans of the game took notice. Once again he buried himself viewing film. "He's always working on something," said fellow Colt Mark Thomas. "He's here early and stays late."[19]

Although Manning's high school did not win a championship and the only title Tennessee won came his senior year when the Volunteers captured the SEC crown, he was still not used to losing and he did not enjoy it one bit. The Colts were still a losing team and that took some getting used to rookie year. Manning also discovered that the NFL operated on a very specific schedule that didn't mesh well with his own nature of being antsy. "I don't throw helmets or chairs after a loss. I don't rant and rave and abuse the media with profanity. I'm more a let's-get-the-hell-out-of-here-and-go-back-to-work guy. But what's frustrating in the pros is that when you lose on Sunday you don't really go back to work until Wednesday," Manning said.[20]

In the NFL Monday is spent watching film and Tuesday is a day off. It is not until Wednesday that teams focus on the following weekend's opponent. So Manning ran up his phone bill calling old friends, his brothers Cooper and Eli, and his old offensive coordinator David Cutcliffe to vent. Then he just went back to work trying to get better and make Indianapolis into a winner.[21]

Despite his pursuit of it, Manning understood there is no such thing as perfection. The funny thing was that if he threw touchdown passes and completed bunches of passes, but the Colts still didn't win, he was a target for wrath. What he never got was how much he was criticized for his peculiar hand motions at the line of scrimmage. It might have been because he made coaches and fans nervous with the play clock ticking down as he tampered with the call. They were sure he was going to incur five-yard delay-of-game penalties.

Manning's gyrations, although they were not for show but for a purpose, never ceased to gain attention from sports writers and TV commentators, as well as fans who called in to sports talk radio shows. Variously, Manning's motions were described as belonging to an "aerobics instructor, a drum major, a disco dancer, a one-man fire drill. His calisthenics continue as the play clock ticks toward zero and the muttering in the stands reaches full roar. Defenses don't like it. Television analysts rail about it. Crowds boil at road games and the catcalls are audible even at home."[22]

The idea behind the demonstrative hand motions is to react to the defensive alignment and if Manning can survey the defense's spread on the field and exchange the called play quickly enough for another that he thinks will work, that is what he is supposed to do. The evidence, right from his first season, is that he possesses the savvy and awareness to do so. If opposing coaches or defenses are thrown off by his arm and hand movements, so much the better. And as far as fans went, no fan was going to boo a first down or a touchdown play.

Manning entered the pro ranks with a sophisticated, prepared, honed outlook that far exceeded what most rookie quarterbacks were capable of and it took only a few weeks for him to dispel any notions that he should ever again be compared to Ryan Leaf. But as he embarked on his pro career, Manning made no boasts and once again turned to his primary role model in his life. If he could just be like Archie Manning, he said, he would be satisfied.

"If I can play as long [14 years] as my father did in the NFL," Peyton Manning said, "plus handle things as well as he did—the media, the fans, the autographs, and do it with class—that will be a real achievement to me."[23]

NOTES

1. "Colts Hire Mora, May Lean Towards Manning," Associated Press (no byline), January 13, 1998.

2. Archie Manning, Peyton Manning, and John Underwood, *Manning* (New York: HarperEntertainment, 2000), 285–86.

3. PeytonManning.com.

4. Don Pierson, "Manning's Experience a Likely Edge Over Leaf," *Chicago Tribune,* April 15, 1998.

5. *Indianapolis Colts 2007 Media Guide,* 97.

6. Hank Lowenkron, "Manning Among History's Top Rookie QBs," Associated Press, December 20, 1998.

7. Ibid.

8. Jimmy Hyams, *Peyton Manning—Primed and Ready* (Lenexa, KS: Addax Publishing Group, 1998), 229.

9. Chicago Tribune wire services (unbylined), February 9, 1998.

10. Andrew Bagnato, "None Finer Than Leaf, Coach Says," *Chicago Tribune,* December 30, 1997.

11. Don Pierson, "Lions' Rookie Outdoing Manning, Leaf." *Chicago Tribune,* October 2, 1998.

12. Michael Ventre, "Beware of Next Ryan Leaf in Draft," NBC Sports, http://nbcsports.msnbc.com/id/7269110/from/RL.5/.

13. Matt Mosley, "Leaf Embraces Place in History," ESPN.com, April 9, 2008, http://sports.espn.go.com/nfl/draft08/columns/story?id=3336006.

14. Lowenkron, "Manning Among History's Top Rookie QBs."

15. Hyams, *Peyton Manning,* 235.

16. Ibid., 229.

17. Mike Chappell and Phil Richards, *Tales from the Indianapolis Colts Sideline* (Champaign, IL: Sports Publishing LLC, 2004), 55.

18. Tim Polzer, *Peyton Manning: Leader On and Off the Field* (Berkeley Heights, NJ: Enslow Publishers, 2006), 71.

19. Joanne Mattern, *Peyton Manning* (Hockessin, DE: Mitchell Lane Publishers, 2007), 21.

20. Manning, Manning, and Underwood, *Manning,* 328.

21. Ibid.

22. Chappell and Richards, *Tales from the Indianapolis Colts Sideline,* 49–50.

23. Hyams, *Peyton Manning,* 231.

Chapter 10

BECOMING THE BEST
IN THE BUSINESS

Peyton Manning was a star from the moment he stepped onto the field to lead the Indianapolis Colts' offense in 1998. But he also realized he still had a lot to learn. He would not have been Peyton Manning if he had wrapped up his rookie season and said, "Good enough." What he did was almost never good enough for Manning. He understood he could always get better and that he could always learn more. If he absorbed more information, then he knew he could call upon this storehouse when he needed it during a tense moment in a game. His long-ago earned nickname of "Caveman," applied by teammates for all of the hours he spent in the dark studying football film, was still relevant.

It didn't take a coach's lecture for Manning to recognize that there were ways for both he and the Colts to grow together. After all, the Colts had not improved by a single game in their record, posting the same 3-13 mark the team had the year before without Manning. And Manning could look at his number of interceptions—that unsightly 28—and grimace.

After a rigorous off-season, Manning felt especially well prepared for the 1999 season. He was no longer a rookie. He had tasted NFL competition and done quite well. Now it was time to show more on the field and to lead his team to more victories. Before the season began Manning jotted down a list of goals that included doing just that—making sure Indianapolis won a lot more than three games that season.

"An athlete has to have goals—for a day, for a lifetime—and I like to put mine in writing so that afterward I can check the design against the finished product," Manning said.[1]

Manning never displayed rookie jitters, but he did display a preternatural calmness his second season, from mini-camps in the spring, through training camp in the summer, and into the regular season. The Colts were also a better all-around team. Bill Polian had acquired a franchise quarterback and set about building around Manning. An important piece of the puzzle was wide receiver Marvin Harrison. A 6-foot, 185-pound end from Syracuse University, Harrison was a two-year veteran when Manning joined the club. Harrison had already showed very positive signs of blossoming into a superstar receiver, but when he and Manning began playing together, they formed a partnership that matured into one of the greatest quarterback-receiver duos of all time. Harrison missed four games of Manning's rookie year but still caught 59 passes.

In 1999 the tandem showed what it could do when all cylinders were clicking and all parties were healthy. Manning and Harrison brought back memories of Joe Montana throwing to Jerry Rice, the most accomplished receiver in NFL history. They developed a sixth sense from practicing and working together, an instinct that appeared to let each player know where the other was on the field at all times. If Manning threw it anywhere close to Harrison, Harrison could grab the ball. In 1999 Harrison caught 115 passes for 12 touchdowns. His catches alone accounted for 1,663 yards. The twosome gave the Colts the deadliest passing game in the league and after a couple of years of floundering at the bottom of the standings the Colts flipped their record around, finishing 13-3, a 10-game turnaround. That was the largest one-season turnaround by any team in NFL history and the Colts won the American Football Conference (AFC) Eastern Division title. At one point Indianapolis won 11 games in a row.

"I sure didn't see us winning 13 games," Manning said. "A 10-game swing isn't something that happens very often in the National Football League and to even suggest it as a game plan is wishful thinking. More dream than scheme."[2]

That type of successful record put the Colts on the map and made the team one to be feared. The 13-3 mark put the Colts into the playoffs and although they lost, 19-16, to the Tennessee Titans, an eventual Super Bowl participant, the season was refreshing for a team short on success in recent years.

In 1998, when Manning was thrown into the first-string job as a rookie, and in 1999, when he had a full season under his belt, he was one of the most scrutinized quarterbacks of all time. Veteran star quarterbacks who had heard so much about Manning as a college player, but not seen as much of him on television playing for the University of Tennessee, brought their curiosity to games when they either got the chance to see him in person for the first time or to play against him. The greats wanted to cut through the hype and form their own opinion about just how good this guy was.

When the Colts faced the Miami Dolphins in 1998, Miami still featured Dan Marino at quarterback. Although the Dolphins won the game, Marino watched Manning throw for 302 yards and a touchdown, in addition to flinging three interceptions. Marino saw the raw goods and pronounced them genuine. "He's got a great attitude, so he's going to be fine," Marino said. "He's going to be a great player in this league. I believe that." San Francisco 49ers quarterback Steve Young concurred with Marino's assessment, saying, "The jump from college to the pros is like going from a tricycle to a car on the highway. It's the speed. When I first started playing I swore there were 30 guys on defense and the field was too small. The important thing is to have a good frame of mind about it.... He seems like the kind of guy who has the mental attributes to pull it off."[3]

It would not be too many years into Manning's Colts career before he was drawing favorable comparisons to Hall of Famers like Marino and Young.

The huge difference in Manning's performance in 1999 was his judgment when he got into trouble being chased by defenders and his vision in seeing how defenders swiftly filled what looked like openings. It might be said that, based on Young's comment, the number of defenders Manning had to contend with shrunk from that fanciful 30 to a real-life 11. The quarterback's newfound experience slowed down the pace of the game.

As a result, Manning's interception total dropped from 28 to 15. The rest of Manning's season-long statistics were stunning. He threw for 26 touchdowns. He completed 331 passes or 62.1 percent of his attempts and his throws gained 4,135 yards, the first of a record six straight seasons in which Manning gained more than 4,000 yards passing. Manning's showing earned him his first trip to the Pro Bowl, the postseason NFL all-star game played in Honolulu. Over the two-year period at the start of his career, Manning also threw a touchdown pass in 27 straight games—that was the equal-fourth-longest total in league history. With Manning at the helm, Harrison retrieving passes, and running back Edgerrin James darting for 1,553 yards on the ground, the Colts had

been transformed into an offensive juggernaut, accounting for a startling 423 points during the season.

"Peyton learned from his mistakes and learned by doing and put up
some numbers that some guys are putting up during their second five
years in the league," said Tony Dungy, who became the Colts' coach
in 2002.[4]

If anyone even briefly thought Manning's starring quarterback performance was a fluke, he put those thoughts to rest immediately with
subsequent years of first-rate showings. Similarly, with Manning as the
leader, the Colts proved that they were for real, that they were building
a team for the long haul, a team that could win every year and that
would threaten to win championships.

"You can't talk about how well things went last year," Manning said
entering the 2000 season. "That's over with. This is all about today.
We're going to set our expectations pretty high."[5]

In 2000 the Colts recorded a 10-6 record and lost to Miami in the
first round of the playoffs. Manning threw for 4,413 yards and 33 touchdowns. He was once again an all-star. He was developing a reputation
around the NFL for being the type of guy who could beat you by himself. With Manning running the show, the Colts were never out of a
close game. He could rally the team to score points in a hurry and the
Colts had the wherewithal to come back in the fourth quarter. Other
teams could never relax in the late going because Manning could
jump-start his offense and drive it the length of the field with only a
few minutes remaining on the game clock. He was the type of player
opponents admired and someone they knew they had to thrust a stake
into his heart to prevent him from overseeing a comeback.

By his third season, Manning was no longer viewed as a newcomer.
He was no longer being compared to Ryan Leaf either, who at the time
was injured and was a member of a winless San Diego Chargers team.
Instead, Manning was being compared to the quarterbacks he idolized
from a distance and whom he had modeled his play on as he was growing up and maturing at Tennessee. It seemed odd for Manning to hear
his name mentioned in the same sentence as perennial NFL all-stars
and he actually told reporters to cool it a little bit.

"After 40 games, he is being favorably compared to the all-time
greats," wrote long-time NFL observer Don Pierson, "a comparison
Manning believes is both unfair to him and the quarterbacks like Dan
Marino and John Elway who excelled for almost as long as Manning is
old." Manning protested his inclusion on such a list of quarterbacks,
noting, "The word 'great' is thrown around too easily."[6]

At the time, Manning admitted that his pregame preparation included staying at the Colts' practice complex until about 9 p.m. each week. "You bust your butt all week for a three-hour game. When you lose, that's why it makes you sick, because you feel like you wasted your time. When you win, it makes you really feel special because you're working for it."[7]

A blip in the Colts' growth occurred in 2001. The team started slowly and finished 6-10. There was a blowup between Jim Mora and Manning after one stinging loss that resulted in an embarrassing public argument. Indianapolis was crushed by San Francisco, 40-21, in a game when Manning threw four interceptions. Mora was furious afterwards and let his emotions out at a postgame press conference. "That was a disgraceful performance ... that really [stunk]," Mora said. "We threw that game away. We just gave it away. I'm not putting it all on Peyton. All I know is we threw four of them. One was returned for a touchdown and the other three gave them the ball at our end of the field."[8]

Manning always took defeat hard and he did not profess innocence. However, he resented being blamed publicly for a loss. Manning felt Mora should have taken him aside for a private chat if he wanted to complain. The way the situation was handled frosted him. "I was fully responsible for that loss," Manning said, "[but] to be called out in front of the whole country, where that press conference is going to be played over and over again, that bothers me."[9]

Manning still threw for 26 touchdowns and 4,131 yards during the depressing 6-10 season, but his interceptions did inch back up to 23. The poor season haunted Mora and he was replaced as the Colts' coach at the end of the year, ushering in the era of Tony Dungy, one that would prove to be the best in Indianapolis history. In 2002 the Colts returned to playoff status with a 10-6 record, though they were smoked, 41-0, in the first round of postseason play. Manning was as good as ever with 4,200 passing yards and 27 touchdowns. His magical link to Marvin Harrison was smoother than ever—they connected on an astounding 143 passes. It was a four-game turnaround for the Colts, but a huge one, taking them from losing team to playoff team. The rebuilding could commence.

The Colts had punctured a tire, but managed to get back on the road. In Manning's five seasons, counting the abysmal rookie year with the 3-13 mark, the Colts had advanced to the playoffs three times. In recent years (far more than in the past), so-called pro football experts have begun to value a star quarterback's achievement almost only by the number of championships he has won. That seems to be the new measuring stick. Quarterbacks compile their 16-game statistics over a four-month regular season, but without help from proficient teammates, they can't control the final act of the season. Despite Manning's magnificent regular-season play, critics popped up saying, "Yeah, but he's never won a playoff game." By the end of 2002, the Colts were 0-3 in their three tries at the postseason under Manning.

"It's not always fair," said Denver Broncos coach Mike Shanahan, "but everybody is evaluated by playoff games. That's just the nature of the system." Manning's voice often sounded weary when he was forced to address the issue and sometimes he even sounded sarcastic. "A lot of times it's the Colts have been to the playoffs three times," he said, "but ol' Peyton, he's 0-3 in the playoffs."[10]

It was not as if Manning was going to give up trying to reach the playoffs year after year. He began each season with optimism, believing that Indianapolis was good enough to keep on playing and winning in January. "Believe me, I wish I could play a playoff game every week," Manning said, "because that's all people talk about: 'When is he gonna win a playoff game?' But the reality is we've got 16 regular-season games to deal with first. If we can take care of the little things and get back to the post-season, I'll take my chances. Trust me—I'd rather be in the arena than be a guy who stops trying."[11]

Not winning a playoff game in his first three tries was portrayed as the chink in Manning's armor. He eschewed the early label of greatness and to prove his point he occasionally talked about Sammy Baugh. Baugh, who died at 94 in December of 2008, is arguably not only the greatest quarterback of all time, but the greatest football player of all time. Baugh was a Texas schoolboy and collegiate legend, matriculating at Texas Christian, who made his NFL debut in 1937. Starring for the Washington Redskins, Baugh helped revolutionize the passing game to make it an equal weapon with the running game. But he also starred as a defensive back and punter. In 1943 Baugh, who threw six touchdown passes in a game at a time when passing was a much smaller percentage of the offense, led the league in passing, punting, and interceptions simultaneously.

Manning met Baugh in 1999 and while Baugh said he would like to be a quarterback in this day and age of the NFL, Manning bowed to the master and said there would never again be a player like Baugh was in the 1940s. "It's pretty safe that all the things he did will never be done again," Manning said.[12]

No one doubts the veracity of Manning's comments on that front. Players no longer compete on offense and defense. Punters and kickers are specialists, not every-down players. The multimillion-dollar invest-ment in quarterbacks prohibits their getting on the field at any other time during a game because of risk of injury, with the possible excep-tion of being a holder on an extra point or field-goal attempt. However, it was apparent that after only a few years as a pro that Manning, too, might do some things on a football field no one else has ever done. Af-ter he had been in the league only a handful of years, statistics showed he was on pace to be an all-time recordbreaker, to crack the marks held by Dan Marino and (in some cases about to be broken) by Brett Favre. They were not one-day performances, but numbers accumulated over time that added up to impressive bodies of work. On the way to retire-ment, if a man was going to reach those numbers, he would have to be great almost every day, almost every game. And even if he would prefer to jettison the use of the word "great," that is what Peyton Manning aspired to—only he viewed it as consistency at a phenomenally high level.

That next level beckoned in 2003. In the final year of his long-term rookie contract, Manning and the Colts were superb together. Manning completed 67 percent of his passes, making two out of every three attempts. He threw for 4,267 yards and hit on 29 touchdown passes while erring on only 10 interceptions in 566 attempts. The Colts fin-ished the regular season 12-4 and as champions of the AFC South Con-ference. Along with Titans quarterback Steve McNair, Manning was chosen as co–Most Valuable Player of the National Football League.

When the playoffs began, the Colts were still hotter than a car engine after running for five hours on a 100-degree day. In a thorough 41-10 dismantling of the Denver Broncos, Manning took care of playoff victory doubters. Moving into the second round of the playoffs for the first time, the Colts outlasted the Kansas City Chiefs, 38-31, in a shoot-out. This set up a confrontation with the New England Patriots for the championship of the AFC and the right to move on to the Super Bowl.

The legend of the new-look Patriots under Coach Bill Belichick and quarterback Tom Brady had not yet been cemented. Brady had assumed controls of the team after starter Drew Bledsoe went down with a seri-ous injury. He had retained control even after Bledsoe got well. Beli-chick was betting that the one-time sixth-round pick out of Michigan, who had been far less heralded than either Manning or Bledsoe in col-lege, was the right starting quarterback at the right time. The Patriots topped the Colts, 24-14, and won their first of three Super Bowls in five years. Brady had begun to emerge as a quarterback whose game and career would be compared to Manning's.

This was the beginning of a new rivalry. From this minute forward, Manning and Brady would be measured against one another for wins and losses and in statistical performance. The rivalry was spiced up because they played in the same conference and neither team could advance to the Super Bowl without defeating the other, and although neither man particularly cared about such things, the starter in the Pro Bowl for the AFC side would almost surely be one or the other. The Patriots had won round one.

There was never any personal animosity on display between the two quarterbacks. They just both burned to win. They were different personalities in many ways. Manning was more of a homebody. He had married his long-time girlfriend Ashley (who stayed as much out of the limelight as Greta Garbo at her most reclusive) and rarely explored nightlife. Brady was single and dated famous actresses and models who had him front-and-center in photographs in the supermarket checkout-line tabloids. Now that Manning had put aside his jinx of not winning a playoff game, the same football observers began carping that he couldn't win the big one over New England.

Manning was invited to deliver a speech at Emory University in 2005 and his talk included a self-deprecating Tom Brady joke. It went like this: Manning died and went to heaven, where he was led to a smallish house with a faded Indianapolis Colts flag flying outside. The house next door was a mansion covered in New England Patriots' decorations and memorabilia. Manning asked God why Tom Brady got such a dream house while he got the shaft. God said, "That's not Tom Brady's house, that's my house."[13]

In early 2003, not long after the 2002 season had ended, Manning became embroiled in an unusual hissing match with Colts kicker Mike Vanderjagt. The place-kicker was quoted by a Toronto television station at a time when his emotions seemed out of whack. Vanderjagt went on the air and criticized Manning and coach Tony Dungy. "I'm not a real big Colts fan right now, unfortunately," he said. "I just don't see us getting better." Vanderjagt felt that Manning did not show enough excitement and that Dungy was too mild-mannered to lead the Colts. "I think you need a motivator, a guy to get in somebody's face."[14] It was an uh-oh, dissension-plagued moment, and Manning did not appreciate Vanderjagt's comments. Manning blasted Vanderjagt for being "an idiot kicker who got liquored up and ran his mouth off."[15] Talk-radio callers and hosts went nuts over Vanderjagt's statements for days, even after he issued an apology. The principals ultimately made peace.

Manning's six-year rookie contract expired after the 2003 season. He had proved to be a superstar who had more than lived up to the Colts' hopes when they made him the number 1 pick in the 1998 draft, and his efforts dictated that he was in line for an even wealthier contract. Manning also had proven to be somewhat indestructible. He had started every single Colts game since he had been drafted. No injury had sidelined him for as long as 60 minutes. One of the more thankless jobs in sports had to be Manning's backup. That essentially meant your uniform would stay free of grass stains forever. You could shower at home instead of in the locker room. This time around Manning signed a seven-year deal for $98 million. The contract included a $34.5-million signing bonus.

Years ago, the phrase "he's playing in a contract year" was spawned for professional athletes whose contracts were expiring at the end of the season. The implication was that they would try harder in order to show themselves in the best light and earn the best possible deal. The additional implication that followed was that such athletes would not be as motivated to play hard once they got their money and settled into a new, long-term deal. Regardless of circumstances, whether he was playing football for free or was compensated with millions of dollars, Manning was not a man to coast. If anything, the general feeling was that Manning *deserved* to be the highest paid player on his team. Manning was the type of guy to take his big salary and use it as motivation to prove that he deserved it by having the best season of his career and leading the Colts deeper into the playoffs and perhaps to the Super Bowl.

From the opening kickoff, Manning's 2004 season was spectacular. His accuracy, efficiency, and throwing prowess boggled opponent after opponent. Fans were giddy. Old supporters just marveled. Manning had reached new heights. Three different times during the regular season Manning completed five touchdown passes in a game. And that didn't count the game when he hit for six touchdown passes (shades of Sammy Baugh). Game after game, Manning rang the bell. He threw for 4,557 yards, a career best, and when the pinball machine stopped rattling around and totaling the points, Manning had completed a new NFL record 49 touchdown passes in a single season. Manning broke Dan Marino's 1984 record by one. (In 2007 Tom Brady broke Manning's record with 50 touchdown throws.)

Manning's record-breaking TD pass won a game for the Colts. He fired the pass to Brandon Stokely for a 34-31 victory over the Chargers. The play was the culmination of an 80-yard drive in nine plays as the clock ran down to 56 seconds remaining. "I think Johnny Unitas would have been proud of that drive," Manning said of the legendary Colts quarterback when the franchise was located in Baltimore.[16]

Manning had a troop of accomplished receivers, but Harrison still shined brightest. One trait common to superstar receivers is their flashiness. In that way, Harrison is their polar opposite. He is quiet and reserved, even if he may be better than all of the others. Colts newspaper beat writers even have trouble pinning Harrison down for interviews except for passing comments. "I just try to make the hard catch routine," Harrison said once.[17]

Harrison, who missed one game that season, caught "only" 94 passes in Manning's outstanding 2004 season. But the Colts had other weapons, so if Harrison was double-teamed the hyper-efficient Manning could make other choices in the secondary, whipping the ball to Reggie Wayne, Marcus Pollard, Stokely, or Dallas Clark. It was further indication that the Colts had the depth of a quality team that might be able to run the table in the playoffs. While there is little doubt that this quality at the receiver position makes Indianapolis a better team, Harrison, like all good pass catchers and runners, always wants more yards for himself.

"I'm never satisfied," he said. "Never, ever. I'm never going to be."[18]

In 2004 Manning was a touchdown-throwing machine. The Colts finished 12-4 in the regular season and again won the AFC South Division while scoring a stunning 522 points, one of the highest totals ever recorded during a single NFL season. There was one particularly entertaining game where Manning and Favre combined for nine touchdown passes and 751 yards throwing in a 45-31 Colts win over Green Bay.

The Colts carried a great deal of confidence into the postseason and after a first-round bye they knocked out the Denver Broncos, 49-24. This once more set up a clash against New England. This may have been one of the most disappointing Colts losses of all. After demonstrating such consistent offensive explosiveness all season, Indianapolis was completely stifled by the Patriots. New England won, 20-3, and went on to claim its second Super Bowl championship of the 2000s.

After the season, Manning was awarded his second MVP award. Only Brett Favre has won three times and Manning joined Unitas, Joe Montana, Steve Young, and Kurt Warner as quarterbacks who had won twice.

"Just being with those names makes it more special and I am very humbled to be on that list," Manning said.[19]

As the 2005 season began, Manning was even hungrier to take the Colts all the way to the Super Bowl. For the sixth straight year he started all 16 games, staying healthy again. His string of 4,000-yard seasons was broken, but that was more of an indicator that the Colts' offense mixed the run in more since Manning attempted more than 100 fewer passes than he did in some of his other top seasons. He still threw for 28 touchdowns, however, with only 10 interceptions.

The Colts posted their best record in the Manning era, finishing the regular season 14-2. Indianapolis was once again king of the AFC South, but in a surprising end to the season the Colts were upset by the Pittsburgh Steelers, 21-18, in the playoffs. It was a game the Colts felt they should have won, and only a few bad bounces cost them. But it was also a game that added to the feeling that the wild-card Steelers were a team of destiny as Pittsburgh marched to Super Bowl victory despite competing in every playoff game on the road.

Manning wondered when it would be his—and the Colts'—turn to hoist the championship trophy.

NOTES

1. Archie Manning, Peyton Manning, and John Underwood, *Manning* (New York: HarperEntertainment, 2000), 350.

2. Ibid., 350.

3. Mike Chappell and Phil Richards, *Tales from the Indianapolis Colts Sideline* (Champaign, IL: Sports Publishing LLC, 2004), 56–57.

4. Ibid., 58.

5. Tim Polzer, *Peyton Manning: Leader On and Off the Field* (Berkeley Heights, NJ: Enslow Publishers, 2006), 82.

6. Don Pierson, "Indianapolis Colts' Third-Year Quarterback Peyton Manning Is Doing—and Saying—All the Right Things," *Chicago Tribune*, November 2, 2000.

7. Ibid.

8. Dan McGrath, "49ers Feast on Five Turnovers," *Chicago Tribune*, November 26, 2001.

9. "Colts' Manning Lashes Back at Coach," *Chicago Tribune*, November 29, 2001.

10. Chappell and Richards, *Tales from the Indianapolis Colts Sideline*, 60.

11. Polzer, *Peyton Manning*, 99.

12. John McFarland, "Slingin' Sammy Looks Back." Associated Press, September 1, 2002.

13. Wire services (no byline), May 19, 2005.

14. "Kicker Criticizes Manning, Dungy," *Chicago Tribune*, January 30, 2003.

15. Chappell and Richards, *Tales from the Indianapolis Colts Sideline*, 114.

16. Don Pierson, "Perfect Time for Manning's Record, 49th TD Pass Keys Comeback Victory," *Chicago Tribune*, December 27, 2004.

17. Chappell and Richards, *Tales from the Indianapolis Colts Sideline*, 75.

18. Ibid., 81.

19. "MVP Goes to Manning in Landslide," *Chicago Tribune*, January 11, 2005.

Chapter 11

DREAMS DO COME TRUE

As defensive players chortled at his line-of-scrimmage hand signals, as football historians pondered his techniques and ability, and as his number of records mounted in the NFL offices, Peyton Manning continued to dream of putting together the perfect season, the one that ended with the Indianapolis Colts claiming the Super Bowl championship.

Before Manning joined the Colts as their number 1 draft pick in 1998, Indianapolis had slumped to a 3-13 record. It is the law of the National Football League that a team must hit bottom—be the worst of the worst—to obtain the top pick in the collegiate draft. From the moment the Colts acquired Manning, the team was on an upswing. Yet at the same time realizing that it takes more than simply a star quarterback to get results in the NFL, the Colts never stopped building, tweaking the lineup, drafting as smartly as they could.

More than once the Colts seemed prepared to make a run at the Super Bowl title. But not even with Manning at his record-breaking best could they make the charge they needed all the way through January and into the first Sunday in February. Whether it was the occasional bad luck, Tom Brady and his Patriots rising to the occasion, or getting ambushed by an unexpectedly sound other AFC team, the Colts had not managed to reach the Super Bowl with Manning at the helm.

So the 2006 season did not initially feel very much different to Colts players than the good starts they put together in some previous seasons. However, by the time Indianapolis was 9-0 the belief was growing not only in-house, in the huddle, but around the league, that this could be the Colts' year. Manning had more weapons at his disposal than ever. The Indianapolis receiving core was deep and talented. There was a question mark in the backfield with the departure of Edgerrin James, but he was replaced by a two-headed monster, Joseph Addai, who rushed for more than 1,000 yards, and his partner, Dominic Rhodes, who rushed for another 600-plus.

With his eye for detail and ability to spot nuance, Manning was more dangerous than ever while changing plays at the line of scrimmage. Even if he did wave and twirl his hands more than Diana Ross and the Supremes, the result was usually quite satisfactory. The Colts employed a quickie, no-huddle offense a higher percentage of the time than other teams because Manning operated it so coolly. He was known for his quick release, for not lollygagging around in the pocket, which put pressure on his linemen to hold their blocks an extra long time. He was not a great scrambler, so he had to spot open receivers fast and unleash his passes swiftly. That became his trademark. Historically, NFL teams used a hurry-up offense only when the clock was running out at halftime or at the end of a game when they needed a fast touchdown. Given that Manning was usually a step ahead of defenses, employing the no-huddle system meant that he could often get off plays before defenses could adapt. The hurry-up kept defenses even more off-balance and gave them less rest between plays. The Colts had a strike-fast offense and using this method they could strike even faster.

It was showtime from the get-go for the Colts in 2006. They beat good teams in close games on the road and ran up bunches of points against weaker teams anywhere they faced them. Reggie Wayne, who made 86 catches, became a favored alternative for Manning's passes when Marvin Harrison was shadowed too closely. Harrison still got open enough to make 95 grabs. Almost everything the Colts tried worked. The season was a joyride.

"We started the 2006 season with strength and promise," said Colts owner Jim Irsay. "Toward the end of the season we hit some bumps. But we never gave up. We didn't listen to those who wrote us off. We never stopped believing that this was our year, that this was our chance."[1]

Addai was under great pressure that season. Manning, Harrison, and James had been called "The Triplets," but James sought a more lucrative deal when his contract ran out and he signed with the Arizona Cardinals. The Colts knew they badly needed to buttress their running game and so made Addai their number 1 draft pick out of Louisiana

State University. The 5-foot-11, 214-pound back had grown up in Houston, and during the second game of his pro career, a 43-24 victory over the Houston Texans, he scored his first NFL touchdown.

The six points came on a 21-yard pass from Manning. What Addai didn't know was that Manning's completion broke the Colts record of 2,796 held by Johnny Unitas. Both players wanted the ball as a souvenir, but Addai had it in his grasp last and didn't seem inclined to let it go. "That's for me," Addai said. "That's my first touchdown. I won't ever forget that one."[2]

Manning actually was unlikely to forget the opening game the week before against the New York Giants. It was the first time he faced his younger brother Eli in a pro contest. The game was hyped ahead of time as "The Manning Bowl," half joke, half facile description. Indianapolis won, 26-21. "I'm glad it's over," Peyton Manning said. "I'm looking forward to some 'regular-season' games. This wasn't a regular game."[3]

Among the victories at the start of the season were a couple of wins against AFC rivals that were important for setting the tone within the division that season. On October 29 the Colts triumphed, 34-31, over the Broncos in Denver. More than 75,000 fans watched Manning's precision throwing pick apart the Broncos. Manning completed 32 out of 39 passes for 345 yards and three touchdowns. Reggie Wayne caught all three. "It's like a playoff atmosphere," Wayne said. "My number was called today."[4]

Denver put a 13-game home-winning streak on the line and rallied to tie the game at 31-31 with 1 minute, 49 seconds remaining. But that left too much time on the clock for Denver to assume Manning couldn't bring the Colts downfield one more time. He did so. Manning hit five straight passes that gained 47 yards to put place kicker Adam Vinatieri into position to win the game. Wayne, who caught 10 passes for 138 yards, was pivotal on that drive, too. Vinatieri kicked a 37-yard field goal to pull it out with two seconds left.

"Great crowd and they've got a great team," Manning said of the then–5-2 Broncos. "Reminded me of Saturdays back in Knoxville."[5]

A week later the Colts met the New England Patriots, their nemesis, at Gillette Stadium in Foxboro, Massachusetts, and prevailed, 27-20. It was the second straight win over the Patriots after nine straight losses in Massachusetts. Some Patriots fans in the stands held up a sign reading, "Manning's A Big Choker." He most certainly was not. Wins over New England were still rare enough to be prized at any time of the season. "We had them in a chase position most of the night," Manning said. "That was part of the plan and it worked out well for us."[6]

Things worked out well for the Colts just about all season. After the electrifying start, Indianapolis did stumble a few times, but finished the regular season 12-4 and as champions of the AFC South. Manning continued to play at a supremely high level, just as he had for several years, making the big plays, coming through in the clutch, piling up the same type of remarkable quarterback statistics. He finished the regular season with 362 completions in 557 attempts for a 65 percent completion rate and 4,397 yards. Manning threw 31 touchdown passes and only 9 interceptions.

The Manning-led offense provided so many thrills for Colts fans that the defense's sometimes erratic play was overlooked. Not when the playoffs began, however. Predictors felt the defense was Indianapolis's Achilles heel and might prevent the team from reaching the Super Bowl.

The Colts opened the playoffs with a wild-card game against the Kansas City Chiefs. Not only did Indianapolis defenders stifle Chiefs star running back Larry Johnson, they limited Kansas City to eight points in a 23-8 defeat. "Our defense did a great job," Reggie Wayne said. "I guess they wanted to shut up a lot of critics."[7]

Victory sent the Colts to Baltimore to face the Ravens. Those aware of the past shook their heads over the irony of this match-up. The Colts, of course, had experienced tremendous glory while representing the city of Baltimore. It was Jim Irsay's father, Robert, who had spirited the team out of town in the middle of the night in 1984 by loading up Mayflower vans with all of the club's possessions. Over the years since Indianapolis had relocated to the Midwest, there had never been as many Colt heroes representing Indiana as there had been Colt heroes representing Maryland. Now that the Colts were poised to bring their first championship to the Heartland, the Ravens (originally the Cleveland Browns and the team that relocated to Baltimore as a replacement for the Colts) stood in their way.

The Ravens, who had won a Super Bowl in 2000, were greatly admired for their defense. The Colts' super offense seemed certain to be tested—and it was. If the players appreciated the Indianapolis defense the week before against the Chiefs, they fell in love with it in a 15-6 win over the Ravens. It took a towering defensive showing coupled with five Vinatieri field goals for the Colts to prevail. "You just feel like [Vinatieri] is going to make everything when he goes out there," Colts coach Tony Dungy said. "In games like this, it's necessary."[8]

Winning two playoff games was nice. It was also necessary. This time the Colts hungered to go all the way, and polishing off two comparatively inferior opponents in the first two rounds was part of what was expected. The wins over the Chiefs and Ravens set up the showdown that NFL fans, TV networks, and, frankly, Peyton Manning sought. Coming at the Colts from the other side of the AFC bracket was the New England Patriots. Again. It was pleasant to beat the Patriots during the regular season, but now it was time to handle them when it mattered most. Thus far, the 2006 season had been satisfactory. The Colts wanted it to become euphoric. They had to dispose of the Patriots in order to make their goals become reality. After disheartening losses to the Patriots in the past, it was time to uplift the team and the franchise by beating New England at the most important time of the year.

The AFC championship game was a home game for the Colts. The RCA Dome was packed with more than 57,000 fans who thought Peyton Manning was a god and that Tom Brady was the first cousin of the devil. The stakes were high. The winner of the game advanced to the Super Bowl to meet the Chicago Bears. The loser of the game went home for the season with many questions floating around as they sat staring into the fire on long winter nights. Colt emotions were taut, but the team was confident and expectant. Then the Colts promptly went out and fell behind 21-3 in the first half.

A lesser team would have died right there, would have rolled over and quit on the season. But the Colts fought back and rallied behind Manning's leadership. They didn't want to be down by 18 points, and so they creatively found ways to score and wipe out the deficit. At that point no other team had trailed by as many as 18 points and come back to win a conference title. By the fourth quarter, the Colts had tied the game, 28-28.

An exchange of field goals knotted the score at 31-31, but then the Patriots took the lead, 34-31, on a Stephen Gostkowski boot, this one traveling 43 yards. Before the kickoff, there were still 3 minutes, 49 seconds remaining. The Colts got the ball deep in their own territory, but Manning crisply moved the offense the length of the field. Finally, Addai plunged over the goal line on a two-yard run, giving Indy a 38-34 lead, but with enough time left for Brady to perform one more miracle. New England began to move. Brady drove his team down the field, but with less than 30 seconds to go, Colt defender Marlin Jackson intercepted a pass.

When the game ended, the 38-34 margin holding up, delirious fans screamed and shouted and so did the Colts. Strips of blue and white

confetti—Colts colors—fell from the Dome roof, half-burying the players in a blizzard of paper. The Colts, not the Patriots, were going to the
Super Bowl this time.

Manning admitted that when the game was tied and overtime
loomed and he had just one more chance to lead the Colts to a score,
he was not only examining the players in his head, but seeking assistance from a higher power. "I don't know if you're supposed to pray for
stuff like that," he said, "but I said a little prayer."[9]

Despite all of Manning's and the Indianapolis Colts' success, to this
point neither had reached the Super Bowl. In postgame interviews,
Manning was asked if he felt he had gotten a monkey off his back by
advancing farther than ever before and if he felt that becoming a Super
Bowl quarterback was a vindication to his career. Out of hand Manning dismissed that way of thinking. "I don't get into monkeys and vindication," Manning said. "I know how hard I've worked this year. I
know how hard I've worked this week."[10]

From all of his experience as an AFC runner-up to the three-time-
Super Bowl champion Patriots in the first half of the decade, Manning
was not about to admit that beating New England was meaningless. He
even confessed to being a little bit scared when the Colts trailed 21-3
and could not make it back to closer than 21-6 at halftime. "You certainly don't envision getting down 21-3 to the New England Patriots in
any game," he said, "much less the playoffs."[11]

When the conference championship games were settled and Indianapolis and Chicago had advanced, it set up the first Super Bowl in
which both teams were led by African American head coaches. It was
Dungy for the Colts and Lovie Smith for the Bears. The two were old
friends and had worked together on the same coaching staff in Tampa
Bay. Each was after his first Super Bowl trophy as a head coach.

"I thank the Lord," said Dungy. "I'm proud to represent African-
American coaches and I'm so proud of Lovie, but this is about Indianapolis and this Colts team right now. I'm so happy Lovie got there
because he does things the right way, with a lot of class, no profanity,
no intimidation, just helping his guys play the best they can. That's the
way I try to do it."[12]

As Manning began practicing for the biggest game of his pro career,
he was nursing a bruised right thumb suffered in the Patriots game. In
the fourth quarter he had banged it against a teammate's helmet. The
thumb had been X-rayed and the pictures showed no break, so he
refused to talk about it anymore. In his entire NFL career, Manning
had only missed one play due to injury. He broke his jaw in a game

against the Miami Dolphins in 2001 while being hit on a blitz. Manning was hoping this visit to Miami for the Super Bowl would be more fun. He was counting on it and dwelling on an aching thumb wasn't going to amuse him much. Instead, he merely told reporters nice things about the Bears' defense, the strongpoint of the NFC champs.

Although that was part of the storyline in the days leading up to what is both the most popular football game in the world and (usually) America's most-watched television show of the year, the other angle that reporters focused on was Manning's presence. After all of his near-misses, Manning was in The Game. The sportswriters wanted to play that up and how much it meant to Manning and how he would feel incomplete if he never won one, but Manning guardedly refused to play the role mapped out for him.

"It's about the team," Manning said. "This is not a personal mission in any way for me. I don't play the 'if you win, if you lose' game. You better try to do it while you have the chance. While we're here, you sure do want to go ahead and win it. I always felt I would have a chance to play in this game. All I knew to do was keep working hard. I certainly would have hoped to have been here earlier."[13]

During that same meet-the-media session that is the staple of the lead-up to the Super Bowl, Manning was peppered with questions from every direction, but he did recount one delightful personal memory in reporting his first encounter ever with a Bears football player. As a four-year-old, he said, while at the Pro Bowl in Hawaii in 1980, he disappeared from his parents' sight for three hours. While they frantically searched for him, he was taking a ride on a catamaran with Walter Payton, who delivered the boy in his arms back to Archie and Olivia. "It's kind of neat to think of that story now that we're playing the Bears this week," Manning said of the late Hall of Fame running back.[14]

The talk leading up to the Super Bowl, as it always does, went on for days, filling newspaper columns and television sports broadcasts, not only in the home cities of the two participating teams, but all over the nation. The day of the Super Bowl has evolved into a national party day that might be on par with New Year's Eve. Instead of Dick Clark and the ball coming down in Times Square, people get to watch Peyton Manning and Bears All-Pro linebacker Brian Urlacher. The difference is that by the time game-time rolls around the contest has been so thoroughly dissected people can't wait for the real thing. The sight of the coin flip to determine first possession is a relief.

When Super Bowl XLI finally began, the Colts were shaken up by the startling Bears' start. Chicago's all-star kick returner Devin Hester took the opening kickoff and ran it back 92 yards for a touchdown, the first time the game's opening kick had been returned for a score in the 41-game history of the championship. But as was their hallmark all season, Indianapolis did not panic. Playing in the rain before nearly 75,000 people at Dolphin Stadium, a poised and artful Manning led the Colts to repeated scores while the formerly criticized defense pressured Bears quarterback Rex Grossman and refused to allow steady gains. The Colts ran up the yards (430) and prevented Chicago from getting its share (265). The final score was Indianapolis 29, Chicago 17.

While Manning manned the offense with 25 completions on 38 attempts for 247 yards and a touchdown, safety Bob Sanders was an all-over-the-field guy on the other side of the ball. Sanders had one interception and forced a fumble. The wet weather made it difficult for runners to hold on to the ball at times. "Everybody did their part," Manning said. "There was no panic, nobody gave up. We stayed calm the entire game. We truly won the championship as a team and I'm proud to be part of it."[15]

Leading up to this game, there had been criticism that Manning could not win the big one to get to the big one. That specious commentary had been put to rest. There were suggestions that the Bears' defense would overpower Indy's offense. Didn't happen. There were long-time observations that the Colts could not win big games unless they had perfect weather conditions like the ones they played in under a roof at home. That argument went down the drain. There were no questions left to ask about a team that deflected every challenge on its way to a Super Bowl crown. "We imposed our will," said Colts running back Dominic Rhodes.[16]

The Colts' window to win a championship seemingly had been open for several years, but never had the right mix of players done it all when they had to in order to win several playoff games back to back. Perhaps the chemistry off the field had not been perfect. Perhaps some little thing always interfered to prevent the franchise from reaching the great goal. The one common denominator in the years leading up to claiming a Super Bowl title was Manning's greatness. Year after year he produced the best statistics and was named an all-star. The Colts won a lot of games, but never enough in the right year. They fixed that oversight during the 2006 season.

It is often said in sports that winning makes everything all right. If there is tension between players and the coach, then winning a title makes everybody happy. If there is tension between the front office and the coach, then winning a title means the coach is retained anyway. If the fans are grumpy about something, they undergo dramatic mood changes if their team wins it all. After all, how bad can anything be if the team keeps on winning and brings home the big trophy at the end of the year?

Tony Dungy not only became the first African American coach to win an NFL championship, he became one of three NFL figures to ever win Super Bowl titles as a player and a coach, joining Oakland's Tom Flores and Chicago's Mike Ditka. An even-tempered, religious man, Dungy was human enough to be disappointed by the Colts' losses, but he never staked his reputation or felt that he needed public validation that he was a good coach if he did not have a Super Bowl win on his résumé. And he felt the same way about his quarterback, Manning, whom he worked with for years, whom he studied opponents with week after week, and whom he observed taking charge in the field and the locker room. Dungy considered anyone who belittled Manning solely because he had not captured a Super Bowl championship guilty of taking a cheap shot and of being ignorant of Manning's day-to-day value.

"Peyton Manning is a tremendous player and a great leader," Dungy said after the Colts won their coveted title. "He prepares, he works. He does everything that you can do to win ball games and to lead your team."[17] In another article he said, "I don't think there's anything you can say now other than this guy is a Hall of Fame player and one of the greatest players to ever play the game."[18]

Keenly aware of NFL history, Manning knew that his idol Dan Marino had reached the Super Bowl early in his career and that the Dolphins had lost. In a long career after that, Marino never got back to the big game. Manning did not want to be haunted the same way. When he was asked after the victory if he took the Colts' accomplishment as a personal triumph, Manning wouldn't admit it for a second, but revealed more of the depth of his thinking in a simple sentence. "I wanted to be on a team that won the Super Bowl," he said.[19]

Indiana is not home to many major professional sports teams. There is no Major League Baseball in the state. There is no NHL hockey in the state. The Indiana Pacers are members of the NBA. The other so-called biggest games, all over the Hoosier state, revolve around college and high school basketball. The Colts had been in Indianapolis for 23 years at the time of their Super Bowl win. Jim Irsay had become owner only one year prior to Manning's arrival. In the glow of the championship, he praised his team of president and general manager

Bill Polian, coach Tony Dungy, and quarterback Manning for making his family's dream a reality.

"The journey was historic and the destination ... it was sweet," Irsay proclaimed.[20]

After the champagne stopped flowing, the parties ceased, and the confetti was cleaned up, the Colts sat back to enjoy the achievement of being named world champions. Within a few weeks after the title was earned, the team announced that Manning was redoing his contract to provide more flexibility in signing players. Manning was due a $10-million roster bonus during the off-season, but by converting it to a signing bonus, the Colts would have more flexibility under the NFL's restrictive salary cap. What this really meant was that the Colts would be able to keep finding new players to keep the team fresh and help make a run at another Super Bowl.

Shortly after the Colts' triumph a humorous aside made national news. A 26-year-old man from Decatur, in downstate Illinois, admitted that he had made a rash bet in a bar to demonstrate his allegiance to the Chicago Bears. Caught up in Super Bowl excitement Scott Wiese signed a pledge before many witnesses that if the Bears lost to the Colts he would legally change his name to ... Peyton Manning.

"I made the bet and now I've got to keep it," the Bears supporter said before he visited a judge to get the legal procedure going to pay off his debt. "I think I kind of represent all Bears fans. Not that they're all idiots like me, but I represent their passion because I really care about my team."[21]

It was not immediately clear if Wiese expected his throwing arm would become stronger as a result of the name change. That did not matter, however. Roughly six weeks later, a judge in district court refused to allow Wiese to become Peyton Manning, worried that it might infringe on the privacy of the real Peyton Manning.

NOTES

1. John Oehser, *True Blue* (Chicago: Triumph Books, 2007), 6.

2. Indianapolis Star writers, *Road to the Championship—Super Colts* (Indianapolis: Indianapolis Star, 2007), 25.

3. "Big Bro Wins Manning Bowl I," *Chicago Tribune,* September 11, 2006.

4. Indianapolis Star writers, *Road to the Championship,* 67.

5. Ibid., 77.

6. Ibid., 86.

7. Doug Hoepker, ed., *Blue Heaven—Indianapolis Colts 2007 Super Bowl Champions* (Champaign, IL: Sports Publishing LLC, 2007), 93.

8. Ibid., 99.

9. Ibid., 105.

10. Indianapolis Star writers, *Road to the Championship*, 189.

11. Ibid., 193.

12. Don Pierson, "Manning's Miracle," *Chicago Tribune*, January 22, 2007.

13. Don Pierson, "Resume Lacks Big Win," *Chicago Tribune*, January 31, 2007.

14. Ibid.

15. Indianapolis Star writers, *Road to the Championship*, 209.

16. Bob Kravitz, "A Day for Manning, Dungy to Stand Tall," *Indianapolis Star*, February 5, 2007.

17. Indianapolis Star writers, *Road to the Championship*, 219.

18. Don Pierson, "Myth-Busting Win for Manning," *Chicago Tribune*, February 5, 2007.

19. Ibid.

20. Oehser, *True Blue*, 6.

21. "He's Got Name," *RedEye*, February 8, 2007.

Chapter 12

FAME, GLORY, AND LITTLE BROTHER

When Peyton Manning walked off the field after his Indianapolis Colts won Super Bowl XLI he had a slight smile on his face. The impact of the long-sought victory did not kick in until a little while later. He partied with his teammates and family and graciously accepted the nationwide praise that accrued to his performance.

But since he was not about to retire, it wasn't long before Manning was back in his "cave" studying film so he could lead the Colts to a repeat at the end of the 2007 season. Winning one Super Bowl was grand, but it remained the goal to cap each professional season. The new season came around quickly enough, within months, with the scheduled mini-camps, training camps, and exhibition games, and then the regular season.

Every professional athlete must come to terms with the march of time. The pinnacle is to achieve the goal of becoming world champion, but the next season always follows, with new members of the team, new teams rising to prominence, and new challenges on the field.

Manning was the rare athlete who would never let a hint of complacency slip into his mind or his performance. He was as hungry as it was possible to be to go out and win a second Super Bowl, and when the 2007 season started it was obvious in his effort and obvious that he wasn't going to permit his Colts teammates to let down either. The Colts showed no signs of weakness and became the first team since the Green Bay Packers between 1929 and 1931 to start a season 7-0 three straight years. As a bonus for Manning, in the seventh win of the

2007 season he broke a hallowed club record. When Manning completed a 59-yard touchdown strike to Reggie Wayne against the Houston Texans, it was the 288th TD toss of Manning's career. That gave him one more than Johnny Unitas had thrown with the Colts.

Manning's skills had been mentioned in the same breath as his idols' for a few years, but he was now starting to catch up to them in the record books. He never changed his demeanor or regard toward those who had inspired him, however. Publicly, he never acknowledged being on the same level of greatness even though evidence indicated otherwise. For Manning, Unitas was on a pedestal and it did not come naturally to the younger quarterback to boast about surpassing the star of the past. "I'm a little uncomfortable talking about the same records he had," Manning said, "but certainly it is an honor."[1]

No one could blame Manning if he had more of a strut in his step. His numbers were proving he was going to be looked at as one of the greatest NFL quarterbacks of all time and his stature as the quarterback of the reigning Super Bowl champions elevated his status even more.

For a couple of years Manning had been in the public eye as a pitchman for various products. Often seen as sober and studious for the devotion he brought to the game, Manning enhanced his image by doing humorous commercials. Now there was also a new aspect to Manning's life in the pros. His younger brother, Eli, had become a member of the New York Giants. Archie Manning's youngest son was now a professional quarterback, too. This created a wide variety of storylines for sportswriters who explored the differences and similarities between the brothers and who enjoyed probing all of the tentacles of a three-quarterback football family.

Oldest brother Cooper and Peyton were close enough in age to overlap for one season in high school where they played pitch and catch for Isidore Newman. Eli is almost five years younger than Peyton, so he never ran with the same crowd. He was the little brother back home too young to go out at night. He was just growing into high school when Peyton was finishing college. So they hadn't even lived in the same house for years.

On the scale of outgoing children, Archie Manning always ranked his boys as follows: Cooper was the most forthcoming and outrageous regardless of public situation; Peyton, definitely more grounded, but with a practical joking side that close friends saw; Eli, quiet, reserved, looking inward, someone who might spend so much time by himself in his room that his parents didn't know he was home. If anything, that may have made Eli the most underrated brother. Outsiders didn't seem to think he had the same confidence as Peyton behind center. He very much kept his own counsel by comparison. Eli described himself as "the shy one."[2]

Peyton and Cooper were old enough to watch their father play professionally, but Eli was just a toddler when Archie retired. There was animated talk around the dinner table in the Manning home, but Eli and his mom, Olivia, did more of the listening than the talking. By the time Eli reached high school age he also showed signs of being proficient in football. When Peyton signed Eli's high school yearbook, he wrote, "Watch out world, he's the best one."[3] No pressure. Years had passed since Peyton went through the public expectations in high school and college, but Eli never felt as if his father would consider him a failure if he didn't become an outstanding quarterback, too.

Peyton had grown up on the lore of the University of Mississippi, drinking in the stories of Archie and Olivia and Saturday afternoon SEC football. He was the one who listened to the old radio broadcasts. Eli had a different upbringing. By the time he became a high school star, older brother Peyton was a national figure playing for the University of Tennessee. Some of the people in Mississippi who had been so rude to Archie and written him off as a traitor because he allowed his son to get away to the Volunteers might even have forgiven him by then. If Eli was an admirer of his older brother he was quiet about it. If Peyton was asked who his favorite football player was, he immediately provided the same answer each time: "It's my little brother," he said.[4] Turns out he had pretty good taste because although Eli had very large footsteps to fill in his own home, he was doing a remarkably good job of it.

When it became apparent that Eli was going to be about as hotly coveted by colleges as Peyton was, it certainly would have been understandable if a feeling of "uh-oh" rippled through the Manning household. But when Eli sifted through all of his offers from all of the schools that sought his services, albeit in a much quieter, somewhat less publicized way than Peyton, he casually informed his parents that he wanted to become a student in Oxford and throw the football for the Rebels. Eli had raised hopes initially by attending a quarterback camp in Mississippi in 1998, but he was being heavily courted by Tennessee, Georgia, Texas, LSU, and Florida, too.

By then, after Peyton's flirtation and alternative decision, the faithful probably were not expecting another Manning on campus. Too much was assumed with Peyton and not enough credence was given to Eli. So his commitment was a little bit of a surprise. One thing that helped sway Eli was the new Mississippi coach. David Cutcliffe had been promoted to the head job. Eli knew how much Cutcliffe had helped Peyton develop and how he had become a family friend. The idea of playing for Cutcliffe appealed to him.

Eli's choice paid all-around dividends. As a player he threw for more than 10,000 yards and 81 touchdowns, led Mississippi to a 10-3 record as a senior, set 45 team or league records, and engineered a Rebels victory in the Cotton Bowl. Little brother also grew up. Things were so hunky dory in Oxford again that Archie and Olivia bought a condominium there to provide a home away from home to use when they traveled to watch Eli's games and to visit him. By the time he was prepared for the pros, Eli stood 6-foot-4 and weighed 225 pounds. Much like his brother, Eli came close in the Heisman voting (third), but was not chosen, though there was not nearly as much controversy. However, he also won the Maxwell Award as the best all-around player in college football for 2003 and the Johnny Unitas Award as the best quarterback that year.

By the end of his senior year at Ole Miss, it was clear that Eli Manning was going to be one of the most sought-after collegians in the upcoming spring 2004 draft. The poor San Diego Chargers, who had suffered through the mistake of trying to turn Ryan Leaf into a pro quarterback, had the number 1 choice in the draft. There was only one problem. Eli, with his father lobbying at his side, told the Chargers and anyone else in the NFL world who would listen that he did not want to play for San Diego. There were some tense moments in the weeks leading up to the draft, with Eli being called "spoiled." But he took his stand and stuck to it, making the Chargers very uncomfortable. The lowly team with the high draft pick that wanted Eli was the New York Giants and that was the team he hoped to play with.

Unbeknownst to most, Giants general manager Ernie Accorsi considered Eli Manning his dream pick. He had been scheming and salivating, hoping and dreaming for roughly a year and a half to plot a way to get this Manning on his team and build around him.

In Accorsi's mind, Hall of Fame–caliber quarterbacks come along only once in a while and are capable, with the right supporting defense, of winning multiple championships. That's what he saw in Eli Manning, not a caretaker quarterback who might win a single Super Bowl if he got lucky, but a future Hall of Famer, a leader of destiny who could carry the Giants to the top several times. "There never was any doubt in my mind about Eli Manning," Accorsi said as he tried to pull strings and create a trade that would bring Eli to New York.[5]

In the end, Eli's reluctance to play for San Diego was a key factor in Accorsi's ability to make a deal. The Chargers asked him to draft Philip Rivers out of North Carolina State with their own number 1, then throw in three draft picks and he had a deal. Accorsi paid the price 'because of his belief in Manning. Rivers became the Chargers' starter and did well, and the Chargers also picked star defender Shawne Merriman, plus two other players. The Chargers did quite well, but the Giants were satisfied. So was Eli, who signed with New York for $54 million spread over six years, including a $20-million signing bonus.

For all of the Giants' belief in Manning, there was no intention for him to become the starting quarterback during his rookie season. For one thing, the incumbent at the time was Kurt Warner, who might have faded a little bit from his prime, but was still a two-time NFL Most Valuable Player. The Giants started 5-2. Manning saw action in a couple of games, including a memorable moment when he was creamed on a hit from Eagles defensive end Jerome McDougle. The monstrous tackle knocked out Manning's mouthpiece (he was crawling around looking for it) and almost knocked Manning out. Archie witnessed the hit and cringed. "I thought he was dead," Archie said.[6]

Eli rose to play again, but when a team slump kicked in, the Giants took the bold step of benching Warner and starting Manning. Although he knew for days what was going to happen, he only told his parents as an afterthought, as in "oh, by the way, I'm going to start," after Archie saw it on the news. That was the blasé side of Eli. He started seven games that season, thrown in much as his brother Peyton had been, but not with the same superb results. If this was a sink-or-swim situation, Eli did no better than prevent himself from drowning. The nine games he appeared in were more for experience.

Expectations did not rise until the next season, though before the 2005 campaign began, the Mannings' home area of New Orleans and the Louisiana Gulf Coast were tormented by the powerful winds of Hurricane Katrina. The quarterbacks lent their support by organizing an empty plane in Atlanta to be flown to Indianapolis, where it was filled with supplies. Then they traveled to the region to hand out goods to residents whose homes had been destroyed and who needed food and other assistance. "The whole town is like family, so it's very much a personal issue," said Peyton Manning. "I talked to the Red Cross and told them I certainly didn't want to get in the way, but I wanted to do whatever I could to help. It's just different when you have your hometown hit. It triggers a nerve."[7]

Eli Manning's second season went much better. He started every game, threw 294 completions, racking up 24 touchdowns and 3,762 yards. However, if he threw an interception at an inopportune time, the Giants Stadium fans let him have it with boos. New Yorkers are not renowned for their patience. It didn't help that Eli's last name was Manning, so football fans just assumed he would be terrific from the first moment he took a snap. Not that his eventual success was doubted in key quarters. David Cutcliffe, who coached both Manning sons, offered a unique take on what made them special, saying they have "functional fast-twitch thinking. I think it's a family trait. I've just never been around people like that."[8] There was a period when fans wished Eli would release the ball faster than he thought, but things were all coming together gradually for him.

As the 2006 season began, both Peyton and Eli were entrenched as the starting quarterbacks for their teams. For the first time they were going to face one another on the field when the results mattered and neither of them relished it. They made it both hard and easy on their parents. It was hard because Mom and Dad didn't want to root against a son and it was easy because at least they could be in one place to watch both boys play. Because the Colts played in the AFC and the Giants played in the NFC, the Mannings would not face each other regularly during the season. At least in concept it was possible for their teams to become champions in each conference and meet in the Super Bowl, but nobody saw the Giants improving that quickly.

The Colts did win their Super Bowl, fulfilling one of Peyton's dreams. Indianapolis wanted to make it two in a row after the 2007 season, but once again their rival New England Patriots were back in the mix, playing out an unbelievable season. Not only did the Patriots win every one of their regular-season games, all 16 of them, a first in NFL history since the schedule had been expanded, but Pats' star quarterback Tom Brady had bested Peyton Manning's single-season touchdown passing mark with his high-flying, high-scoring offense. Brady threw for an astonishing new record of 50 touchdown passes in a season.

Indianapolis was tough during the regular season but, given the Patriots' nationwide attention, compiled a 13-3 record somewhat removed from the spotlight. Then the Colts stumbled in the first round of the playoffs, losing to San Diego, 28-24. The season ended much earlier than Peyton Manning had expected.

Meanwhile, in the NFC, the Giants, who had barely qualified for the playoffs, were catching opponents by surprise. After a 10-6 regular season, the Giants defeated Tampa Bay, the Dallas Cowboys, and the Green Bay Packers, all on the road, to shock America and reach the Super Bowl. By then the Patriots were 18-0 and simply awaiting coronation.

In a shocking upset, however, Eli Manning and his teammates had every answer they needed. As Peyton watched from a luxury box where TV cameras caught him fretting and rooting for his brother, the Giants shut down Brady and his passing game and kept constant defensive pressure on the Patriots. Still, with the clock running out, New England led 14-10 and seemed likely to survive. But on a crucial play Eli Manning faded back, dodging tacklers, pulling away from one who had a grasp of his number 10 jersey, and threw downfield to tightly covered receiver David Tyree. Tyree made a miraculous catch, grabbing the ball with one hand and holding onto it by pressing it against his helmet as he fell to the turf.

"David Tyree put some stickum or something on his hands," said Giants linebacker Antonio Pierce. "That was special."[9]

That play set up the winning touchdown in a 17-14 game and the Giants were NFL champions. In an improbable circumstance, one year after Peyton Manning was chosen MVP of the Super Bowl, Eli Manning was selected as MVP of the Super Bowl. "It's just surreal," Eli said of the confluence of circumstances.[10]

Until that moment, Eli was by far the lesser known of the Manning quarterbacking brothers. In the glitzy, hype-driven world of the twenty-first century it is almost impossible to be out of the limelight in New York, but there was no doubt Eli was in the shadow of Indianapolis-dwelling Peyton. As he became a bigger and bigger star, Peyton had become a tremendously well-recognized advertising icon. When he was named MVP of the Super Bowl, Peyton's fame only grew. But when Eli was named MVP of the Super Bowl, advertisers leapt in and enjoyed pairing the brothers together in commercials.

As a child and teenager in New Orleans, Peyton was the serious, introspective brother. Cooper craved attention and engaged in pranks and jokes fearlessly. When they were both in college, if Cooper was mistaken for Peyton he didn't confess. Instead he would sign autographs as his brother and perhaps even tell an unsuspecting fan that he was going out to get plastered at a bar the night before a big game. As Peyton aged he became a little bit more outgoing, willing to participate in pranks. After several years of success in the NFL, Peyton, again viewed as staid, serious, and perhaps even aloof, willingly participated in a makeover of his image, letting his inner comedian come out.

A few years ago, Manning parodied both his own reserved image and sports fans in a series of "everyman" commercials. In one commercial, as he watches meat cutters slice up their products he cheers, "Cut that meat!" He stands nearby rooting on movers as they load trucks. As a piano slips away he tells them not worry because the fans aren't booing, they are shouting, "Mooovers." When a paper boy smashes his front window with a delivery, Manning, standing outside in a robe sipping coffee, tells Johnny it's okay, that he still has the best arm in the neighborhood. The counterintuitive campaign was a smash hit, accompanied by comments such as "Who knew Peyton Manning had such a great sense of humor?"

Long committed to community service and raising money for good causes, Manning proved he was perfectly content in his own skin by hosting *Saturday Night Live* and participating in skits that made fun of his own public image. During his monologue he spoofed his mother as the only non-football player in the family. Manning said with a look of fake disdain, "She never made it to the NFL. Got cut by the Dolphins. Tried Canada for a bit. She's a real disappointment for all of us." One routine in particular had football fans holding their sides and produced coast-to-coast commentary. In a parody of the National Football League's United Way campaign with players, Manning played himself teaching children how to run pass routes. When they failed, he screamed at them, he clobbered one kid with a throw to the head that sent him to the turf, and then he flirted with a mother on a nearby bench. The theme of the fake commercial was essentially "Spend time with your kids so Peyton Manning doesn't." It brought down the house with the SNL audience, if only because Manning had come off previously as some sort of ideal, a man whom you would trust your kids with to do anything and be gentle and nurturing with them.

In 2007 Manning attended a state dinner at the White House for England's Queen Elizabeth II. Among the other guests at the white-tie gala were golfing legend Arnold Palmer, former Secretary of State Henry Kissinger, and former First Lady Nancy Reagan. No one reported Peyton drawing up pass routes on linen napkins.

Peyton and Eli began appearing in commercials together. Actually, Archie, Peyton, and Eli appeared in one of the "Got Milk?"–themed commercials as far back as 2004, but the pace increased. For the television sports network ESPN they were portrayed—with Archie—walking down a hallway at the network headquarters receiving a tour from employees. Peyton begins bullying his younger brother by flicking his fingers against the back of his head. Eli comes back with a slap to the back of the head. As Dad turns around to admonish them, Peyton shrugs and points at Eli. Then, as the picture fades, Peyton kicks Eli in the butt.

They also appeared together in commercials touting the arrival of the 2008 NFL season on TV and in a faux debate with Venus and Serena Williams, the tennis champion sisters, over who would beat the other set of siblings in a newly invented game, the Double Stuf Racing League (essentially an Oreo cookie–eating competition, or rather an Oreo white icing–licking contest). Eli gets the punchline after the Williams say they are going to wipe the floor with the Mannings. Just like kids, Eli says, "Oooh, we're scared."

A public service message on urging parents to read to their kids featured Peyton, Eli, and Cooper, the latter two sharing the bottom of a bunk bed with Peyton on top, as Archie reads a bedtime story.

In another NFL commercial leading up to a Colts–New Orleans Saints game, Peyton Manning checks into a hotel at the same time as Saints star Reggie Bush. They immediately get on the telephone and send fake orders to the other's room through room service. Peyton orders 10 lobsters to be sent to Bush's room. Bush orders a 30-foot po' boy sandwich sent to Manning's. At the end, with a cow walking in front of his bed, Manning says, "It is so on."

In a short period of time, it was fair to say that Peyton Manning had transformed his image from somewhat of a geek to perhaps the funniest man in sports. On a Chicago sports talk radio show, Marc Silverman, one of the hosts, admitted to a man-love crush on Manning based upon his football achievements and off-field performances combined. "He's a cool guy," Silverman said.[11]

Even before he won the Super Bowl MVP award, Eli had endorsement deals with Reebok, Toyota of New Jersey, and Citizen Watch Company. Peyton had already been an endorser for MasterCard (which featured a round of Priceless Pep Talks from him during an entire NFL season), DirecTV, Sprint, Gatorade, Reebok, and Xbox. *Sports Illustrated* estimated that Peyton was raking in $13 million a year from off-field product endorsements.[12]

Like any wise quarterback, Manning treats his offensive linemen well. They play the most anonymous positions on the field, yet the quarterback's success and well-being depend on their blocking. A few years ago Tom Brady did a commercial where his linemen were at a dinner table in full uniform making comments. Highly paid quarterbacks have been known to treat their linemen to Rolex watches and the like. Manning used his pull to get his linemen into a DirecTV commercial, but took some teasing abuse from them anyway. All-star center Jeff Saturday joked, "He acts like he did a great thing getting us in the DirecTV commercial, but he didn't get us speaking parts. We're looking for speaking parts. We're looking for the attention to be focused a little more on us and a little less on him."[13]

Even the byplay between the brothers themselves seemed to graduate to a new level now that Eli had taken his team to the top, too. Leading up to the Super Bowl, Eli joked that when he played football with Cooper and Peyton as a little kid all he got to do was center the ball. Peyton was the quarterback and Cooper the receiver. He teased that maybe now he could be a receiver, too, in family games. Peyton said Eli's performance rated more than that. "I guess I'll have to let him throw a few now," Peyton said.[14]

One other activity the family engaged in as a team was a quarterback-coaching camp called the Manning Passing Academy. It would be hard to beat the credentials of a camp that included Archie, Peyton, and Eli Manning as counselors if you wanted your son to earn a college scholarship, go on to the pros, or just make his high school team. Eli's stature was a bit bigger when he showed up for quarterback camp in July of 2008 than it had been before. He might no longer be the third listed name on the marquee. Since the end of the Super Bowl in February, Eli had gotten married, visited the White House as a guest of President George W. Bush, and even played a round of golf at St. Andrews, the home of the sport, but Archie did not believe the rock-solid youngest son seemed any different. "Eli's not going to change," Archie said.[15]

Still, July was not as kind to the Mannings as one might have expected. Much like he had suffered right before the end of his career at Tennessee, Peyton was afflicted with an infected bursa sac. This time it was his left knee. He underwent surgery in late July and missed all of the Colts' training camp. The rarely injured Manning had never missed a regular-season NFL game and he promised that he would not this time, either. The Colts projected that Manning would return to the lineup in four to six weeks, which would be either right at the end of training camp or at the beginning of the regular season.

"I experienced some swelling during the off-season, but it didn't cause me to miss any sort of workouts," Manning said after the condition became known. "I had a great off-season as far as weight lifting. My throwing, my running and my conditioning were as normal as in past years. I was controlling the swelling with treatment and occasional draining."[16] But then the injury worsened and he realized the pain was caused by an infection.

The Manning brothers' national profile was never higher as the 2008 season began. The commercials were part of it and so was the fact that the two men had each taken their team to Super Bowl victory in the last two seasons and each had come home carrying the MVP trophy. For Peyton, questions revolved around how quickly he could play at full strength given that he was missing so much practice time. In all, over the summer, Peyton missed 35 practices and three exhibition games. It was unusual that there were any questions about Peyton since year after year he had shown up, thrown the heck out of the ball, led his team to the playoffs, and been selected for the all-star team. For Eli, the question was whether he could keep up the great run he had used to lead the Giants through the playoffs, if the "real" Eli had emerged and maturity had taken hold.

Answers came quickly and positively about Eli. The Giants got off to a swift start and assumed the lead in the NFC's Eastern Division. Indeed, it seemed as if Eli had become the NFL quarterback Ernie Accorsi and others expected.

Peyton Manning pronounced himself fit for the season opener, September 7, 2008, marking the debut of Lucas Oil Stadium, a new home for the Colts, against the Chicago Bears. "I'm glad this day is finally here," he said.[17] Then the Colts went out and were manhandled by the underdog Bears, 29-13. The game showed that neither Manning nor his club was in mid-season form and the feeling continued through a sluggish first couple of weeks.

Surprisingly, Peyton Manning and the Colts were struggling for the first time in years. Information about Manning's injury and recovery were guarded with the zeal of the Army protecting the plans for the D-Day invasion. Some of the stealth information was revealed after the season began when sports writers learned Manning had had a second surgery as a "cleanup" part of his rehab.

"I don't think it set him back," Colts coach Tony Dungy said. However, Manning did admit after the Colts defeated the Baltimore Ravens, 31-3, that missing practice time might have affected him early in the season. "I've been working through that," he said.[18]

For so long Manning had been the indestructible quarterback who never skipped a snap, so adjusting to have to rebuild trust in his body was a new experience. And he was not the only one on his team with health issues. The Colts had a multitude of injuries. Their offensive line was in shambles and with Peyton's condition being suspect, he found it more difficult to elude the rush and get off his passes with the same accuracy. Yet it was understood that as the season went on,

as the Colts players returned to full strength and when Peyton Manning returned to being 100 percent Peyton Manning, the operation
would be back in gear. Signs of the old Manning were on display in the
fourth week of the season. For most of the game against the Houston
Texans, the Colts were mired in the same type of out-of-kilter play that
had characterized the first month of the season.

Houston led by 17 points and it appeared as if Indianapolis was on
its way to an ugly 1-3 start. However, in the final four minutes–plus
Manning and the offense clicked into gear, scoring 21 points for a
31-27 victory after the situation looked hopeless. "It didn't look good,"
the Colts quarterback said. "You're watching the clock and you sort of
do the math and you say, 'It's going to take three scores. Are we going
to have time?'" As had become typical over the years, Manning made
time.[19]

John Madden, the Hall of Fame coach who won big with the Oakland Raiders and became more famous as a broadcaster, long ago
observed what set Manning apart as a player for the ages. "Peyton
Manning just continues to amaze me with what he's capable of doing,"
Madden said. "You go to practice and you see him doing exactly what
he does in the game. Everything is thought about."[20]

As the knee heeled and Manning's timing came back, the Colts rallied. The Patriots were catching the Colts at the end of October, con-
tinuing their storied rivalry, and even the usually taciturn New
England coach Bill Belichick was effusive about what Manning has
always been able to do and still could do. "He does everything well,"
the three-time Super Bowl–winning coach said. "He makes all the
throws. He is smart. He reads coverages extremely well. He is accurate
with the ball. He is mobile enough in the pocket to buy time. He really
doesn't have any weaknesses."[21] And that from a coach who has been
Manning's rival for years and watched him on film more than an addict
to a 24-hour cable movie channel.

Manning did improve week by week during the 2008 season, leading
Indianapolis to a 12-4 record after the slow start. He also once again
passed for more than 4,000 yards and threw for 27 touchdowns. His
sterling performance, especially bouncing back from serious injury, led
to Manning being named the Most Valuable Player of the NFL for the
third time.

There is every reason to think that Peyton Manning will keep on
completing passes for the Colts for years to come and that within a few
short years he might well be in position to break the NFL's all-time record for touchdown passes thrown and for most yards gained. Along

the way, the boy who grew up dreaming of becoming a champion National Football League quarterback might yet win another Super Bowl or two.

He would blush if anyone said it within earshot and the words would never tumble from his own lips, but the longevity that piled up year after year with the accompanying statistics accruing on his resume and honor after honor being bestowed on him indicates just one thing. Someday soon, and certainly after he retires, one of the most precious descriptions of all will be shouted in the NFL world: Peyton Manning is the greatest quarterback of all time.

NOTES

1. "Manning: Slow Start, Then Mark," *Chicago Tribune*, October 29, 2007.

2. Ralph Vacchiano, *Eli Manning: The Making of a Quarterback* (New York: Skyhorse Publishing, 2008), 23.

3. Ibid., 26.

4. Ibid., 37.

5. Ibid., xvi.

6. Ibid., 89.

7. Marsha Walton, "Manning Brothers Team Up for Katrina Relief," CNN.com, September 5, 2005.

8. Andrew Bagnato, "Eli Manning, the Youngest of Mississippi Legend Archie Manning's Three Sons, Is Starting and Starring at Quarterback for the Rebels," *Chicago Tribune*, October 16, 2001.

9. Tim Layden, "They're History," *Sports Illustrated*, February 11, 2008.

10. Ibid.

11. Marc Silverman, "Waddell and Silvy" radio show, ESPN radio, January 31, 2008.

12. Pete Donohue, "Eli Manning's Super Bowl Performance Makes Him a Household Name," *New York Daily News*, February 5, 2008.

13. Terry Bannon, "Linemen Make Prized QB a Believer," *Chicago Tribune*, February 2, 2007.

14. "Eli Keeps Super Bowl MVP Award in Family," Associated Press, February 11, 2005.

15. "Super Bowl Ring Won't Make Eli Different Manning," Associated Press, July 13, 2008.

16. John Clayton, "Manning Will Need 4–6 Weeks to Recover from Knee Surgery," ESPN.com, July 24, 2008, http://sports.espn.go.com/nfl/news/story?id=3504073.

17. Michael Marmot, "Colts Acknowledge Manning Had Second Knee Surgery," Associated Press, October 14, 2008.

18. Dan Pompei, "Manning Is Back, Loaded for Bear," *Chicago Tribune*, August 27, 2008.

19. Phil Richards, "Colts Convert Texans' Generosity into Critical Victory," *Indianapolis Star*, October 6, 2008.

20. John Madden, "No Surprises from Vikings, Colts," AllMadden.com, November 9, 2004.

21. "Numbers Aside, Manning Still One of the Best," Scout.com, October 30, 2008. http://nwe.scout.com/2/806533.html.

Appendix

PEYTON MANNING'S PROFESSIONAL QUARTERBACK PASSING STATISTICS

Year	Attempts/ Completions	Yards	Touchdowns	Interceptions
1998	575-326	3,739	26	28
1999	533-331	4,135	26	15
2000	571-357	4,413	33	15
2001	547-343	4,131	26	23
2002	591-392	4,200	27	19
2003	566-379	4,267	29	10
2004	497-336	4,557	49	10
2005	453-305	3,747	28	10
2006	557-362	4,397	31	9
2007	515-337	4,040	31	14
2008	555-371	4,002	27	12

SELECTED BIBLIOGRAPHY

BOOKS

Chappell, Mike, and Phil Richards. *Tales from the Indianapolis Colts Sideline.* Champaign, IL: Sports Publishing LLC, 2004.

Hoepker, Doug, ed. *Blue Heaven—Indianapolis Colts, 2007 Super Bowl Champions.* Champaign, IL: Sports Publishing LLC, 2007.

Hyams, Jimmy. *Peyton Manning—Primed and Ready.* Lenexa, KS: Addax Publishing Group, 1998.

Indianapolis Colts 2007 Team Media Guide.

Indianapolis Star staff. *Road to the Championship: Super Colts!* Indianapolis: Indianapolis Star, 2007.

Lowenkron, Hank. "Manning Among History's Top Rookie QBs." Associated Press, December 20, 1998.

Manning, Archie, Peyton Manning, and John Underwood. *Manning!* New York: HarperEntertainment, 2000.

Mattern, Joanne. *Peyton Manning.* Hockessin, DE: Mitchell Lane Publishers, 2007.

Mattingly, Tom. *Tennessee Football—The Peyton Manning Years.* Charlotte, NC: UMI Publications, 1998.

Oehser, John. *True Blue.* Chicago: Triumph Books, 2007.

Polzer, Tim. *Peyton Manning: Leader On and Off the Field.* Berkeley Heights, NJ: Enslow Publishers, 2006.

Savage, Jeff. *Amazing Athletes—Peyton Manning.* Minneapolis: LernerSports, 2005.

Stewart, Mark. *Peyton Manning—Rising Son*. Brookfield, CT: Millbrook Press, 2000.

Vacchiano, Ralph. *Eli Manning: The Making of a Quarterback*. New York: Sky-horse Publishing, 2008.

WEB SITES

AllMadden.com
ESPN.com
NBC Sports, www.nbcsports.msnbc.com
PeytonManning.com

VIDEO

Colts' Road to XLI. Post-Season Collector's Edition DVD. NFL Films, 2007.

ARTICLES

Bagnato, Andrew. "None Finer Than Leaf, Coach Says." *Chicago Tribune*, December 30, 1997.

Bagnato, Andrew. "Eli Manning, the Youngest of Mississippi Legend Archie Manning's Three Sons, Is Starting and Starring at Quarterback for the Rebels." *Chicago Tribune*, October 16, 2001.

Bannon, Terry. "Linemen Make Prized QB a Believer." *Chicago Tribune*, February 2, 2007.

"Big Bro Wins Manning Bowl I." *Chicago Tribune*, September 11, 2006.

Clayton, John. "Manning Will Need 4–6 Weeks to Recover from Knee Surgery." ESPN.com, July 24, 2008, http://sports.espn.go.com/nfl/news/story?id=3504073.

"Colts Hire Mora, May Lean Towards Manning." Associated Press, January 13, 1998.

"Colts' Manning Lashes Back at Coach." *Chicago Tribune*, November 29, 2001.

Donohue, Pete. "Eli Manning's Super Bowl Performance Makes Him a House-hold Name." *New York Daily News*, February 5, 2008.

"Eli Keeps Super Bowl MVP Award in Family." Associated Press, February 11, 2005.

Freedman, Lew. "QB on Pace to Make History." *Chicago Tribune*, November 22, 2004.

"He's Got Name." *RedEye*, February 8, 2007.

"Kicker Criticizes Manning, Dungy." *Chicago Tribune,* January 30, 2003.

Kravitz, Bob. "A Day for Manning, Dungy to Stand Tall." *Indianapolis Star,* February 5, 2007.

Layden, Tim. "They're History." *Sports Illustrated,* February 11, 2008.

Madden, John. "No Surprises from Vikings, Colts." AllMadden.com, November 9, 2004.

"Manning: Slow Start, Then Mark." *Chicago Tribune,* October 29, 2007.

Marmot, Michael. "Colts Acknowledge Manning Had Second Knee Surgery." Associated Press, October 14, 2008.

McFarland, John. "Slingin' Sammy Looks Back." Associated Press, September 1, 2002.

McGrath, Dan. "49ers Feast on Five Turnovers." *Chicago Tribune,* November 26, 2001.

Mosley, Matt. "Leaf Embraces Place in History." ESPN.com, April 9, 2008, http://sports.espn.go.com/nfl/draft08/columns/story?id=3336006.

"MVP Goes to Manning in Landslide." *Chicago Tribune,* January 11, 2005.

"Numbers Aside, Manning Still One of the Best." Scout.com, October 30, 2008. http://nwe.scout.com/2/806533.html.

Pierson, Don. "Indianapolis Colts' Third-Year Quarterback Peyton Manning Is Doing—and Saying—All the Right Things." *Chicago Tribune,* November 2, 2000.

Pierson, Don. "Lions' Rookie Outdoing Manning, Leaf." *Chicago Tribune,* October 2, 1998.

Pierson, Don. "Manning's Experience a Likely Edge over Leaf." *Chicago Tribune,* April 15, 1998.

Pierson, Don. "Manning's Miracle." *Chicago Tribune,* January 22, 2007.

Pierson, Don. "Myth-Busting Win for Manning. *Chicago Tribune,* February 5, 2007.

Pierson, Don. "Perfect Time for Manning's Record, 49th TD Pass Keys Comeback Victory." *Chicago Tribune,* December 27, 2004.

Pierson, Don. "Resume Lacks Big Win." *Chicago Tribune,* January 31, 2007.

Pompei, Dan. "Manning Is Back, Loaded for Bear." *Chicago Tribune,* August 27, 2008.

Richards, Phil. "Colts Convert Texans' Generosity into Critical Victory." *Indianapolis Star,* October 6, 2008.

Silver, Michael. "Peyton's Place." *Sports Illustrated,* Super Bowl XLI Commemorative Edition, February 2007.

"Super Bowl Ring Won't Make Eli Different Manning." Associated Press, July 13, 2008.

Ventre, Michael. "Beware of Next Ryan Leaf in Draft." NBC Sports. http://nbcsports.msnbc.com/id/7269110/from/RL.5/.

Walton, Marsha. "Manning Brothers Team Up for Katrina Relief." CNN.com, September 5, 2005. http://www.studentnews.cnn.com/2005/US/09/04/mannings.relief/index.html.

INDEX

About the Author

LEW FREEDMAN is a Chicago-based sportswriter and the author of 35 books. His other Greenwood titles are *LeBron James: A Biography* and *African American Pioneers of Baseball*. Freedman is a graduate of Boston University, has a master's degree from Alaska Pacific University, and has worked on the staff of the *Anchorage Daily News*, the *Chicago Tribune*, and the *Philadelphia Inquirer*.